<u>Back To My Beginnings</u>

<u>A Memoir by Paddy Staplehurst</u>

There is no universal truth! There is only the truth each of us holds in our heart. Sometimes my truth may touch another's heart, sometimes another may recognise my truth, but each one holds their truth in their heart.

This is a true story, but some names have been changed to ensure privacy.

My sincere and heartfelt thanks to my friend and mentor, Roger M. Allen without whom this book would have never been finished.

This book is dedicated to my sister Dawn, my husband and friend Michael, my dear son Peb, his wife Tarnya, my lovely granddaughters, Yasmin and Danielle, and my grandsons, Callum, Marc and Vincent

St. Etheldreda's Home The Sisters' Front Door

The Chapel

Back to My Beginnings

List of Photographs

Chapter 1: Back to My Beginnings

She closed the door behind her and walked slowly into the summer sunshine, hampered by her " new" suitcase. She felt unreal; surely this wasn't the end, just this! Walking away after twelve years, the "good-byes" and "good lucks" still ringing in her ears, and she just walking away. She struggled down the imposing front steps, which were wide, white and curving to embrace, enfold the front door, well one of them anyway, though the other door wasn't really the "front door", merely a small, modest exit or entrance which happened to be sited at the front of the large house, the sort of door every other house had. The Front Door had a brass, shiny letter box and a large impressive brass knocker which resounded echoingly through the "Sisters' hall". This was a huge, barn-like, though very grand, front hall reserved exclusively for the nuns who ran St Etheldreda's or "The Home" with the bleak efficiency which seemed to rule out love, human or God's. She remembered one night, but…..

She passed the arid flower beds where the snowdrops clustered thickly on dark January days, but which lay barren for the rest of the year, shaded as they were by the bushes and shrubs which gave this part of the front garden a dark, forbidding air even in the bright summer sunshine, but that was yesterday, last week, last month, last year, last decade, last… She remembered… but that too was yesterday. Now she was free, now she could walk in the sunshine, could… But what could she do? She passed her tree, a big plane tree which was visible from several view points around the small market town. It towered above the other trees and she remembered…but she must look forward, forward to an exciting adventure, a future, but of what? Thirty girls plus staff had surrounded her always, or it seemed like always, and now, here she was completely alone. She'd gone to bed with the other girls,, woken by the bell, done her "job", tidied her bedroom until summoned by another bell, she'd gone to the refectory for breakfast…she'd never really been alone, never made any real decisions and now she was completely on her own !! What was she to do? How would she know what to do?

She finally reached the big green gate, not the Sisters' smaller gate some twenty yards up the road, but the large double - barred gate. She put down her suitcase while she manipulated the latch which was difficult as it was and had been broken for as long as she could remember it. She slipped through the gate and, as she was refastening it, looked once more at the place that had been her home for the last twelve years; a home, a prison, a place to flee to from the jeers of the derisive school children, delighted to have someone more unfortunate than themselves to mock, a place to flee from to the freedom of academic work, such as it was. Then, against her will, she was carried away and lost in a flood of memories so vivid she almost relived the misery, the sad and lonely years. She didn't think of them as such, but that was because they had not been interspersed with moments of companionship and communion with others. Paddy was not to realise for many years that to feel desolate one must also have felt happiness and companionship; when one had scaled the heights, one could almost welcome the sadness, and the loneliness of human existence as humankind can only identify moments of despair because of moments of joy. But now her mind fled back through time, through the long barren years, till suddenly she almost cried out in fear.

The Plane Tree in the Front Garden of the St. Etheldreda's Home

The chapel is on the left and Holy Trinity church is behind the tree.

Chapter 2: Crime and Punishment

Paddy woke with a start! She could feel them. They were back again! The worst things she could think of! They must be snakes, as when the Sisters spoke of the Garden of Eden, they always spoke of the terrible snake that had caused Adam to be cast out of Eden, so she knew they were the most terrible and frightening things in the world. Snakes…they were back again; they could not be heard, but she knew they were there. They were under her bed! Paddy listened intently, but only the horror of the night sounds came to her straining ears. She identified the noises, which came straight out of a nightmare delirium.

Thud, thud, thud; that was the sound Donna's head made as it hit the wall behind her bed; first to the left, then to the right, thud, thud, thud, left, right, left right, like some dreadful army that marched with Donna all and every night. Paddy could imagine the snakes writhing to and fro in time to Donna's ghastly music, thud, thud, and thud. In the daytime, she envied Donna with her long, golden curls and pretty doll-like face, marred only by her crooked nose. She had come with the Christ Child, but unlike the smooth baby face of the Christ Child in the crib, Donna's face hadn't looked very nice. It was all battered and bruised and bleeding and her nose stuck out at a funny angle. Her terrible face and matted hair spoke of a lifetime of living and dying. Paddy wondered how someone as happy as Donna in the day-time could spend her sleeping hours each and every night reliving her former life as she banged out the agonies of her parents' sins.

There were other sounds too in the dreadful darkness. She tried to calm her loudly beating heart, shut out Donna's mad music and listened intently once more. There was Moira whimpering. Paddy remembered Moira coming to the Home too. Paddy was proud of the fact that she and her sisters had come here as the very youngest. She thought she could remember walking to the Home because there were two ladies, one of them dressed rather like a witch, all in black; she'd envied her little sister, Bille because Bille was only holding the hand of one of the ladies while she was in the middle, but she couldn't remember walking. The ladies kept talking and she was pushed to the front, as if she were in a pushchair. They had come when they were two and three respectively and she had been at the Home the longest, well her and her younger sister, Bille.

Paddy sighed when she thought of Moira: She had a sister called Janet and she was here too, but Moira was a bully. Paddy avoided her; she hid from her. Moira would bite, scratch, pinch or punch the little ones and she would smile that terrible smile while she was doing it!. She hated Moira, but you had to do what she said; one day she would not, but that was some way off. Moira was just a little bit older than Dawn, Paddy's eldest sister, but she was much bigger than Dawn. Moira was Dawn's best friend, but she even hurt Dawn sometimes. There were the most terrible fights between them and Paddy was frightened for Dawn. Moira would go very red and her pale blue eyes would snap and her ugly mouth would smile and everyone was frightened. She was a big-built Teutonic girl who seemed to have little inner peace and was always fighting. Moira was cold and unfeeling throughout the day, but in the nightmare hours, when the snakes and other, as yet undiscovered, horrors stalked the Home, Moira would cry and whimper just like the girls would if they encountered Moira during the day when she went about her terrible business.

A sharp cry split the whimpering and thudding and everything ceased as if the very air held its breath. Paddy immediately identified the source; it was Bille, her little sister. She was calling for her mother. She called to Bille in a stage whisper, telling her it would be all right; Mummy would be here soon. Paddy knew she wouldn't, but she also knew from three long years' experience that Bille never wanted or remembered her mother in the waking hours. Bille had been here since she was two and during the day she no longer remembered or even thought about her mother and neither did Paddy. Paddy searched her memory for a face, a scent, anything…but there was nothing. Bille had come to the Home with her, but they had both been too little. She remembered sitting under the school-room table and banging their heads on it in the rare moments when Dawn managed to get them out for meals or bed. Dawn told her they had stayed under the school-room table for a long time until Paddy's legs were working and then they went to the school in The Crescent; the three of them were the only girls in the Home to go to this school and they danced and painted, played and listened to stories. Paddy had liked that school, but after a few short months they didn't go any more and had to stay in the Home. She considered why this was for a moment and then, dismissing the problem, turned her thoughts to Bille once more. Bille had short blue-black hair and boot-button black snapping eyes; she was never afraid of anything and had lots of friends. People liked Bille because she was the youngest and because she was so naughty and because she was always laughing, but Bille called for her long forgotten mother in her sleep and only Paddy knew, but couldn't help.

The thudding continued, but Moira had stopped whimpering. Paddy listened with her whole body. Yes, they were still there. She heard a new sound - slip slop, slip slop- that was someone coming down the stairs from the "big girls" dormitory. She listened even harder, knowing she would eventually recognise the footstep. It was funny how in the nightmare hours you could recognise people from all sorts of noises that you never heard in the day. She went back to her listening and then gave a broad smile in the darkness: yes it was Joyce. She almost laughed out loud and the snakes hastily retreated. Joyce! Paddy loved Joyce; Joyce was always happy; Joyce wasn't afraid of snakes, she wasn't afraid of anything. She sometimes even thought that Joyce didn't know the snakes were there.

Joyce had a glass eye to protect her. She put her eye in a little box every night and walked in her sleep every night too amongst the nightmares and the snakes. Why didn't she fall down the stairs? Why didn't she know about the snakes? Paddy had thought about this a great deal and had decided it was because of her glass eye. What a lovely thing it was to have a glass eye. She wondered if Joyce would let her see her putting her eye in the next morning. She had done once. Paddy could still remember it. Joyce had washed the eye first and Joyce had let her hold it. It was like a big marble with a big eye painted on it and it was heavy and cold. Joyce could not hold her empty socket open long enough to show her the hole, but Joyce held the washed marble in her hand, flung back her head and there it was! It glared balefully at you, never moving. Paddy wondered if Joyce put her eye in before she went walking. If not, how did it protect her? She considered this gravely, then smiled to herself in the darkness, a smug self-satisfied smile; that was it, she thought. Just having one protected you. It really must be a wonderful thing to have a glass eye and Paddy wondered how Joyce got it. She must ask her and perhaps she could get one too. The slip slop died away; the night was quiet once more. The snakes had fled with the sound of Joyce's footsteps and had not reappeared. The dormitory too was hushed and silent.

Paddy listened to the silence and faintly heard the familiar sound of Maggie calling her cats. "Toni, Toni", the cry became louder. The cats' names were Sheila and Tommy, but Maggie was not only deaf, she also had a speech impediment. Maggie was short and plump and had very little hair; a hairnet covered the little she had. She had been badly burned in a fire, which had robbed her of her hearing and most of her hair and also left her practically unintelligible. She cooked and washed at the Home and loved her cats. She called them her bubbies. Maggie had always been at the Home; her whole life revolved round her cats, the Deaf and Dumb club and "her" kitchen. Maggie called Paddy, Parly and she lived in a sort of no-man's land, being neither staff nor a child and eating all her meals in the kitchen, even on Christmas day! Maggie was a sort of absurd "Cinderella" with her cheap scent and garish jewellery, which she wore when she went to the club. You couldn't really love Maggie, as she was difficult to get to know and she didn't speak to many of the girls, but she liked "Parly" and had taught her the Deaf and Dumb language. Paddy lay in bed moving her fingers deftly as she went through the alphabet from A to Z. She thought of Maggie being marooned by her tragic circumstances and physical disabilities. Maggie lavished all her love and her affection on her cats. She wished she could have a cat, something to love. Something Paddy could call her own, out loud so people would know it was hers. Maggie's cats were enormous. Tommy was ginger and white, a tomcat who sang dolefully when the moon was at its fullest. Sheila, who Maggie said had been "done", was black and white and was even bigger than Tommy; in fact she was easily the biggest cat Paddy had ever seen, even bigger than the Cheshire Cat in "Alice through the Looking Glass", though Sheila didn't have the same malicious grin The cats lived in the laundry room in two enormous baskets and they sometimes allowed her to stroke them. Maggie's voice died away and all was quiet once more.

She felt the night close in on her. Get out of bed, the voice ordered her. She wished she had done when Joyce was slip slopping on her nightly promenade or even when Maggie's strangely comforting voice had echoed through the silent garden, but she hadn't. She had just decided to start the long trek to the toilets through the endless, eerie and unlit corridors and stairs when a dreadful scream rang out bringing the snakes out once more from the terrible world they inhabited into the night-mare reality of the dormitory. She froze. Who screamed? She peered into the inky black darkness, but could see nothing. Was it Daisy or Janet? Paddy listened intently. Nothing except for the rhythmic sway of the snakes as they swept the dormitory floor in search of...Her mind flicked back to the scream; was it Rachel? Paddy didn't know. She lay still, the terror of uncertainty receding while the night became silent once more. Paddy thought back to when the lights were switched out a few hours ago. Dawn had sung "Eternal Father strong to save". Dawn would often sing for her before they went to sleep, and she knew that when Dawn sang, although the whole dormitory could hear, she really sang only for her. Paddy knew it was true because Dawn always sang her favourite hymns. It was very strange that when she went to sleep, she didn't feel alone because of Dawn's singing: she felt a real part of her sister, but when she woke up to the night sounds, they were so very different from the singing and therefore it seemed much worse.

In her mind Paddy went through the deaf and dumb language once more and then tried words instead of mere letters...Maggie had been kind to teach her. She trembled with pride when she remembered that she had been the only one to learn it. She loved learning something new. She was halfway through the second sentence when she heard a mad despairing cry. Paddy identified it immediately as Betty. Betty always gave this loud scream, then sat up, shouting something about a bomb, and then lay down again. She remembered she'd asked Betty about the bomb in the sunshine hours, but Betty looked blankly at Paddy and asked "What bomb?"

Paddy thought about the words of a Christmas carol, the one which went: *Silent night, Holy night, all is Peace, all is quiet"*, but she knew the night was a time for horror which is why people slept and why the sun turned its face away and couldn't bear to look. No one else knew; they all slept. Paddy wondered why she didn't sleep and instantly knew the answer. She was dirty and smelly and wouldn't get out of bed…that reminded her of her problem. She must get out of bed, but the snakes were still there.

Paddy decided to solve the problem "logically". It is very difficult to be logical when you are only six, but she tried. What would happen if she didn't get out of bed? She would be whipped…whipped. What a funny word that was: "whip". It didn't really mean whipped; it meant you were hit very hard on your bare bottom with the back of a large wooden hair-brush several times. You were hit as hard as Sister Maud could hit you and it hurt! If she didn't get out of bed and brave the long dark corridors and flights of stairs to the toilet, if she couldn't move through the snakes, this would happen to her. She would first of all have a cold bath. She would have to lie in a bath full of cold water for fifteen or twenty minutes, depending how much time there was; you were only allowed two or three minutes for a normal hot bath and Paddy had been taught when she was very young the exact amount of water she could have and the exact procedure you had to follow when bathing. This procedure was designed to give you the cleanest body in the minimum time using the least amount of water: five minutes was considered the absolute maximum time which could usefully be spent in the bath, though the average time was half that. As she was dirty and smelly she had to learn two procedures, the one for a normal hot bath and the one for a cold bath. For a cold bath, you had to lie in the bath and have enough water for you to be almost fully submerged in the cold, cold water; she was then whipped and then she then had to go through the humiliation of being scorned and ridiculed by everyone when Sister Maud announced it to the whole community at morning prayers in the Chapel. She knew all this and she only had to get out of bed and walk, but the snakes………She couldn't imagine what would happen to her if the snakes got her. What did "snakes" do? She knew what they did in the Bible, but here and now? She could never think beyond the snakes. She lay there, willing herself to get out of bed when another chilling scream rang out and that decided her; she turned over, the bed went cold and wet and she slept.

Next morning passed as she had predicted, but the horrors of the night had been dispersed with the sun's powerful rays and Paddy had forgotten them. She could not understand why she had not simply got out of bed and walked along the corridor and down the stairs to the toilet. The nuns told her she was dirty and smelly, so she accepted the cold bath, the whipping and the public denunciation of her "crime", and the ridicule and the scorn with the meekness born of knowing that one's punishment is the result of perfect justice. "I'm just a dirty, smelly home kid," Paddy whispered to herself. "In fact, I'm the dirtiest, smelliest Home kid here."

Chapter 3: Lost and Found

There was some excitement; Joyce was missing, Joyce, with her happy nature and her glass eye, her magic eye! Why did she think Joyce's eye magic? Paddy didn't know. She felt she knew something about Joyce's disappearance, felt she knew that Joyce was all right, and felt she knew where she was. Had she dreamt it? But if she had, why couldn't she remember the dream? Even if Paddy had been asked she wouldn't, couldn't remember where Joyce was or how she knew. She was puzzled. She seemed sometimes to know more than the other girls, but she could never remember how she'd acquired the knowledge.

Apparently Joyce had gone to sleep in her bed last night, but was not there in the morning. Girls and staff were rushing about in a panic, but Paddy didn't seem to be concerned and yet she loved Joyce because she had a glass eye. It was big and round and shaped like a marble, and the eye just looked at you in a benign manner; never looking cross or angry. Paddy realised suddenly that Joyce never got cross or angry either, and even though she was a "bigun" she was still kind to the "littlies". Perhaps it was because she had a glass eye that she couldn't get cross, as it would look very funny if one eye looked cross and the other one didn't. Paddy giggled to herself at the picture in her mind of Joyce trying to look cross whilst her glass eye smiled. She wished she had a glass eye; the wish had a familiar ring about it, but she couldn't remember wishing it recently. She dismissed yet another problem from her mind and turned her thoughts back to the missing Joyce. Joyce had curly hair too. Real curly hair, not just the rag curls the "biguns" sometimes did, even though it was not allowed; Miss Howkins then had to wet their hair to get the curls out before they went to school. Joyce had curly black hair and Joyce sometimes let her touch it or even brush it.

Paddy came out of her reverie to find everyone still searching for Joyce. Voices were calling everywhere. By now the search had become more organised and after a thorough search of the top floor, it had steadily and methodically filtered down to the lower depths of the house and penetrated the Tube. Paddy shivered as she thought of the Tube. It was a long dark passage that ran the whole length of the house. The Home was actually two houses which were joined by a very long underground corridor called the Tube. It ran underground and was punctuated by several alcoves or huge cupboard-like structures that had no doors, but ran into one another; they were always inky black, but they must have had some lights in them. Paddy was to discover the lights years later as the switches to the lights in the "tube" were too high to reach. She, like most "littlies", seldom went there voluntarily, as not only would the "biguns" hide in those dreadful alcoves and grab you as you ran terrified down the long, long darkness, but even when she knew the "biguns" weren't about, she felt a cold, sick horror whenever she entered it. Paddy had counted the steps from the kitchen where the Tube started to the Laundry room where it ended and it was over 100 of her steps. After 80 you could call out to Miss Darnell, the lady in charge of mending and altering of dresses; she worked all day in the laundry room and then went home to her sister at night. Miss Darnell could hear you so you were safe. For the first 15 steps the light from the kitchen lit the way so again you were safe, but the 65 steps in between were fraught with danger.

They had found Joyce curled up in the Laundry basket. She was safe and still asleep. Paddy tried to find out if Joyce had her glass eye in, but no one would tell her. She was desperate to find out, but couldn't think of why it was important. Paddy thought she half remembered asking that question before, but that was impossible, as Joyce hadn't ever been found in the Laundry basket or been really lost before. Why did she keep thinking she remembered things others didn't know? She gave up the puzzle and remembered with pleasure when she too had slept in the laundry room.

A long time ago, everybody had slept there. It was fun and the girls' bodies were warm and you felt you belonged. Paddy had slept on the ironing table and it hadn't mattered a bit when she fell off, as Sister Maude had just picked her up and placed her between her two sisters, Bille and Dawn. The snakes had gone and the horrific noises were quieted too. There were other noises, bangs, whistles and crashes and every where was dark; not the evil darkness of the Tube, but a cosy mole-like darkness which everyone shared, and the bangs and crashes were in the sky and couldn't touch her.

The warmth of humanity spread its soft, safe blanket over and around her; she woke to the soft murmur of voices and someone making soothing noises in her ear. The staff and girls were united in a common bond against the loud cacophony in the sky and when Paddy woke in the night, she lay listening to the regular breathing of her sisters, and their close comforting smell and touch and was at peace. She had no cold baths, no whippings and no fear. She reached out in the night hours and touched them; she was secure and safe. They didn't sleep there now and Paddy was fearful. Perhaps that was why Joyce had come down to sleep in the laundry basket, but Joyce was always happy, Joyce had black curly hair and a glass eye.

Paddy remembered the funny boxes they had to carry to school. She hadn't had to carry one, as she didn't go to proper school; she and her sisters went to school in The Crescent where they did painting, drawing and dancing. None of the other girls went to that school, only her and her sisters and she loved it. She loved the "kindergarten" as it was called, because everyone was very kind and there was a lovely warm smell. When they came home, they all had a sleep in the nursery. There were big shutters, which closed and, if it was sunny, you could put your hand up to the sunbeams, which crept through the nooks in the shutters and you could see your blood in your hands. Paddy loved that. She did have a box with her name on it that hung in the Tube. The Tube was not frightening at that time; it was their playroom and although she could find an empty cupboard-like room to dream in, she could still hear the warm sounds of companionship as they percolated through the thick walls and, as there were no doors, she could catch glimpses of Maggie and Miss Daniels as they went about their daily business.

It was funny how things changed and as they changed they seemed less sure, less positive. Then the clamour or the War as the grown-ups called it, was outside, above them and everyone protected her from the enemy, the thing behind the noises, the horror as they called it; but the horror wasn't there, or if it had ever been there it was now exorcised by their kindness, by their care. Now the noises were inside, were a part her, of them, of the Home, part of their very being and Paddy seemed to be the only person who knew it. They, the night noises, invaded her cocoon of loneliness and they made her do wicked, dirty things; they created the snakes and on Sundays when Father Hankey spoke of "Hell on earth" she knew it was real. The snakes were real and they were here! She thought it strange that the other girls and the staff and sisters couldn't hear the night noises, couldn't hear the clamour, sense the snakes or know and feel the real horror. They just punished her, ridiculed her, whipped her and scorned her.

Paddy remembered even further back when she wasn't here, but……where? She forced her mind backwards into the abyss. She tried, but could find nothing concrete, just separate images…. Paddy thought there were some stairs, but no banisters. No real banisters and the stairs were narrow and seemed to go up and up with just one bend in them. There were no landings; the stairs and walls were made of wood and she, Bille and Dawn would play "witchy" up and down the stairs. She thought she remembered Bille always lost; her legs were too little…Had they really played "Witchy" or was it a dream, and the night noises just a delirium, a nightmare? Was it real? And if they had played it, surely she must be able to remember how to play it; Paddy seldom forgot anything and yet it was all gone, all gone. She couldn't remember.

A solitary tear fell in mourning for her lost childhood, her inability to relive, a pang of loss as she half glimpsed the laughter she had once been part of. Where had it gone? Paddy didn't laugh with her sisters now; she didn't laugh like in those far off happy times. She tried with all her might to picture the carefree days she'd once lived, to take hold of those dream-like days, which she thought may have been her reality just three years ago. Paddy gave an involuntary chuckle as she thought she saw in her mind's eye a picture of her and Dawn being pursued by poor Bille whose despairing cry of "wait for me" always heralded her actual appearance. Paddy had belonged to the other world, the lost world, but she had forgotten how to play "witchy". In fact she didn't play now, not really play, not proper play as she was sure she and her sisters had played in that other world, her lost world; not how she and the other girls had played when they lived in the Tube.

It was difficult to remember that now, that time in the Tube; yet that had been just a little time ago, before Donna and Moira came, but still not that long ago. Paddy had been here a long time she thought with pride, longer than anyone else in the dormitory, except for Dawn, and she didn't count. Why didn't she play anymore? Perhaps Home kids didn't play; yet she hadn't always been a Home kid; Paddy thought she must be very wicked. "The sins of the fathers shall be visited on the children". She knew they said that in church; Paddy could recite most things they said in church. She didn't have any trouble in learning the collect. Each week after church all the girls over the age of seven had to learn the collect for that particular Sunday; Paddy wasn't seven yet, but she still learnt it although she wasn't tested. She thought about the "sins of the fathers", but she didn't have a father, so it couldn't be that. Paddy was pleased that wasn't the reason for her wickedness; *The mills of God grind slowly, but exceedingly small.........*was from the Bible too. It meant that she would be punished for everything she had done. What had she done? Why was she always dirty and smelly now? She had cold baths and whippings every morning, but Paddy still couldn't - wouldn't - go to the toilet. She was easily the dirtiest, smelliest "Home kid" there was; her sisters didn't do it. Why did she?

A bell faintly penetrated her silent reveries; Paddy came back to reality with a start. The breakfast gong reverberated; it was called the bell, but it wasn't really a bell. She sat up quickly and suddenly realised she hadn't done her job. Every morning, in common with the other girls, she had her job to do. Woken at 6.30, they had to get up and make their beds, tidy their dormitories, and then do their job before breakfast at 7.30, and she hadn't done it! Paddy couldn't remember anyone not doing it at all, but she couldn't do it now; it would take too long to sweep the Sisters' landing and dust it, which was her job for this week. Some girls did their jobs badly and didn't pass Sister Maud's inspection, but no one had ever simply refused to do it. She would be punished again, but what that punishment would be, Paddy didn't know. No one had ever missed her job except this dirty smelly home kid. Why was she dirty? Why didn't she do as the other girls did? She gave a big sigh, squared her skinny shoulders and went down to face the inevitable. God sees everything you have ever done wrong and some day you would be punished she thought. That day had come!

Chapter 4: Buttercups and Daisies

Paddy eyed the autumn leaves hopefully; perhaps today would be the DAY!! If it were to happen, it should be today, as conditions seemed absolutely right. There was a very gentle breeze, not the strong gusting wind that made it impossible to judge exactly where the leaves would flutter to earth. She had never caught one, but today…It was difficult to catch one when you were free, but when you were confined within a "crocodile"!…She must not leave the rigid double line which made up the "crocodile", but the leaves danced and whirled to the right and left, front and back of her, but never within her grasp, imprisoned as she was in the crocodile, within the constricting confines of the Home. Paddy looked wistfully at the other children going to school; they were not shackled to the crocodile. They were in ones and twos experiencing their absolute freedom, but without the knowledge or understanding of that freedom. Paddy thought how sad it was that knowledge only came when you were different; when you didn't or couldn't have things others took for granted. She looked with amazement as the brightly coloured "good-luck charms" fell within the grasp of the "other" children, unhampered as they were, but they didn't appear even to see the leaves and failed to appreciate the potency of them, let alone catch them.

Paddy knew only two ways to achieve good luck: one was to catch a falling leaf before it danced to the ground and the other was to find a four-leaf clover. She also knew the leaves were the easier of the two as she had spent all her spare time in the long summer holidays searching for a four-leaf clover without any success. She pondered as to why the "others" refused the undoubted good-luck the leaves would bring; perhaps they didn't know that the leaves were lucky? This was so dreadful, it wasn't possible: to be able to reach out your hand and grasp all the good-luck you would ever need and not realise…no, there had to be another reason. Suddenly Paddy knew the answer…of course; it was only "dirty smelly Home-kids" who needed the charms. The children of freedom had so much they had no need of leaves or clovers; they were free. They were clean. They were the "others". Paddy thought of a world where children who needed charms found it impossible to get them, and children who didn't need them could have them for the asking.

The crocodile stopped to cross the road, abruptly it seemed to her lost in her own private world, and she bumped into the girl in front who kicked her. This brought her sharply back to reality and Paddy saw, with startled delight, she was already at the "plant lady's". The lady was very old, older than Sister Evelyn, the oldest nun in the Home, who was brought out of her bedroom on special occasions, clean, with pink cheeks, white whiskers and faded blue eyes; she was arrayed in her best habit to preside over the proceedings like the "best" dolls on the Sisters' landing. They were called "best", but in fact were the only dolls Paddy had ever played with and they were kept in a large chest for 363 days of the year. They were only brought out on one or two days of the year and then only played with by one or two of the girls; one could go five or six years without seeing them. The dolls were never allowed to be taken beyond the small stairs at the top of the Sisters' landing. Dawn said the Canadian Air Force had given the dolls to the three of them, though why the Canadian Air Force should do such a thing, she didn't know. However, she could remember the three of them going to a big hall, the biggest she had ever seen with an enormous number of men all dressed the same, and being given the most beautiful doll she'd ever wished for, but whether it was real, she didn't know.

The "plant lady" was not stored away, but with round, brown, boot-button twinkling eyes and white hair which gleamed and sparkled through the lattice work of a thick hair-net, she would fuss over her plants, while her equally antiquated husband would mend the shoes brought to him by all and sundry. Paddy looked immediately to the window,. Although it was a cobbler's shop, it was the plants that dominated the small window; they were all succulents, Miss Howkins had told her. Paddy had designated one corner of the window each day to observe the progress of each and every plant. She could never stop, propelled as she was by the momentum of the crocodile, but she always positioned herself carefully in the crocodile before she left the Home, so she could take every opportunity to check all the plants were growing and progressing satisfactorily. Paddy looked at the day's appointed place and saw, with a surge of happiness, that some of the plants had been rearranged to make way for a new-comer; it was very small and had three fat, green fingers pushing their way upwards from the brown soil. Just like the three of them Paddy thought. Bille was the youngest and smallest in the Home and this plant was the smallest in the window ; Paddy liked things to "fit", as it were..

Paddy's smile became even broader as she passed Joe, the only black man to live in the busy market town. He was a taxi driver and once, on an errand for Sister Maude, she had stopped and spoken to him. Paddy couldn't speak when trapped in the crocodile, only if she was on her own, which didn't happen very often; somehow when you were in a crocodile, you couldn't live outside yourself, you could only live inside. Joe seemed to understand and it was an unspoken agreement between them, so opportunities to chat were few and far between. He had come to the Home to take the Reverent Mother to the station and Paddy had crept into the front garden, which was absolutely forbidden, to talk to him. She had discovered he had two daughters, Edith and Theresa and Edith was a nurse. Paddy often saw Edith and smiled at her, but she loved Joe best and this morning he seemed to crinkle up with laughter as if he knew all about the new plant too. His black face, different from the coal-man's although they were both black, seemed to light up with the absolute joy of living and his conspiratorial morning wink appeared even more special.

Paddy skipped through the school gates, one of her favourite places. She was free from the restrictive crocodile. She giggled inside and a smile beamed to most of the school children. Although she was a "dirty smelly Home kid" she didn't mind, as she thought it was true. Paddy loved school, but didn't like Miss Daniels, the Head Mistress, because although she had a round, jolly face, white hair and glasses and a big smile, Miss Daniels herself wasn't in that smile. Paddy walked through the "big ones'" playground; "the little ones'" school was behind the big ones,, so the little ones had to walk further. The school day began with Assembly which she liked; all the children sat on the floor in rows that were determined by class, which in turn was determined by age. The big children who sat at the back were nearly ready to go to the big school. Paddy was halfway and she was also the middle one of three sisters; this was nice as it matched: she liked things that matched. Paddy loved the songs they sang at assemblies and as she stood up to sing the one chosen for this morning, she realised it was her favourite:

Buttercups and Daisies,
Oh, those pretty flowers
Coming in the spring-time
To give us happy hours

Paddy almost bubbled up with the excitement of singing her song, her favourite. The song finished and everyone sat down, but she was savouring the words of the song. Buttercups, what sort of flowers were they? What did they look like? She loved words, loved how the sound of them gave clues to their meaning. She liked the puzzles and riddles contained within the words and how the addition or subtraction of a single letter could change the meaning. "Butter", butter like marge, but more so. Paddy had seen pictures of butter in the "King asked the Queen, and the Queen asked the Dairymaid" book at school, and it was thick and yellow. "Cups", well everyone knew what they were, you drank from them, so buttercups were bright fairy cups which grew in fields of laughter and picnics...She had been for a picnic once, walking past the school and up the hill, though not as far as the Isolation Hospital. Dawn, her eldest sister, had been in the hospital for a while with Scarlet Fever; Paddy wondered whether Dawn hadn't touched her collar when she saw an ambulance. *...never swallow, never catch a fever*
Not for you, not for me,
Not for all the family"

At the picnic they had sticky orange drink. They had picnicked in a magical golden field so thickly carpeted with buttercups, it looked as if it belonged to King Midas; she knew about him from a book she'd read at school. The flowers seemed to ring with gaiety and they showered golden drops of pollen all over them. The bees buzzed with contentment and the smell of new mown hay from a neighbouring field made her head swim in the giddy drunken stupor of the real joy you felt when you were perfectly in tune with the natural world.

Paddy saw the two oak trees in the middle of the field, felt the coolness and tranquillity of the paler flowers beneath them and experimented by sitting first in the shade of the massive trees and then in the bright, golden light streaming from the sun and the buttercups. In her mind, Paddy switched from the golden, magical day to the last line of the song, *"To give us happy hours"*. Yes, that was it! She knew! Paddy had been there and it was true. A feeling of excitement welled up within her; she wanted to dance and shout her truth. That was how word puzzles were solved; you simply thought of the words and then you solved the puzzle. The words were true and she had done it! That was why the song ended like that. The person who had written the song knew about the picnic; everyone had picnics like that; everyone, whether you were called a dirty smelly Home-kid or were someone like Sherry who lived in a real home and went to dancing lessons and wore lovely clothes and had curly hair, you still belonged, you were still a part of everyone. She looked round for someone to share this amazing discovery and suddenly became aware of a silence, stretching like a barrier between her and the rest of the school; Paddy was once more marooned and isolated from her fellows. Everyone was standing up!

She scrambled to her feet and hid her face, wondering if her faux-pas had been noticed. Lifting her head after a while she felt the baleful, stony stair of Miss Daniels and knew she'd been found out. Why didn't the other children have these problems? Paddy had been late for breakfast, hadn't done her job, had been dirty and now hadn't been paying attention and had been found out! Perhaps other children didn't "know", didn't have the joy of discovering how things were, perhaps they didn't think, but as Sister Maude would say, that was "unthinkable!" Paddy chuckled in her mind as she described the fact that children who might not "know" were unthinkable. What do other children do inside their heads when they don't think? She pondered on this problem until once more she was snatched back into reality by the child next to her poking her in the ribs. The assembly had finished and the school were filing out. Paddy turned to the child behind her and smiled gratefully, tripped over the step and followed her class into morning school.

Chapter 5: Christmas Is Coming

It was nearly Christmas! Paddy knew because of the changing hymns in church and the changing collects. They had *ploughed the fields and scattered* and given *voluptuous praise* to *the saints who from their labours rest*; they had *kept the church with Thy perpetual mercy* and been *granted the grace to withstand the temptations of the world, the flesh and the devil* and had now arrived at "Stir up Sunday". She loved this Sunday. The girls, as usual, had gone to church two by two in a crocodile; boys weren't allowed at the Home and the Home girls felt superior to them, especially the Barnardo kids who were rowdy and loud. Paddy knew this as they had once gone to a big party with the Barnardo children and the Home-kids had just stood around whilst the Barnardo kids had raced about, chasing each other and were so noisy that you couldn't hear the adult who was in charge! It was "Stir up Sunday", and Bille, who was not considered either old enough or good enough to go to church, had pleaded with Sister Maude to let her go. Bille's pleading was a force to melt the strongest opposition; her liquid black eyes spilled over with "real" tears and Sister Maude capitulated.

But Bille was bad! Bille had planned her surprise attack with almost pitiless precision. She asked Sister Maude if she could sit at the end of the pew, the seat by the aisle, so she could see more clearly. Sister Maude was swept away by Bille's enormous eyes and made the mistake of thinking that such a touching request, to actually want to go to church, not the normal reaction of most of the other girls, was the mark of a truly saintly child. Sister Maud forgot completely the premise of original sin and willingly agreed. Bille waited her chance. This came after the Creed and during the main prayers, when the nuns would be at their most pious and therefore at their most vulnerable, and then she struck! She toddled up the aisle as fast as her four year old legs would carry her and chaos followed in her wake and reigned supreme. The chanting of prayers faltered, the nuns were jerked violently from their peaceful and spiritual meditations to the reality of Bille's evil and unprovoked attack on law and order, dignity and tradition. Bille was in the chancel and her element; her small fist tugged experimentally at the beautiful alter cloth, leaving well-sucked and dirty finger marks on it, and then proceeded to investigate the priest's costly and elegant cope.

Father Hankey was nonplussed. He, first of all, ignored Bille, as one would a small dog that has misbehaved by leaving a rather unwholesome reminder of his presence behind. But Bille was not a small dog! She had been taught by that hard master, experience, that you had to keep trying if you wanted to accomplish what you set out to do; she was also blessed or cursed, depending on which point of view you held, with enormous reserves of persistence and was, therefore not to be ignored. Bille gave a hard tug to his girdle; Father Hankey frowned and tried to shake her off, but Bille was not to be shaken off either. The churchwarden tried to protect his master from this dastardly attack, and crept forward as surreptitiously as possible. Bille, seeing a potential playmate in this unlikely specimen, joined in willingly. She chuckled as she played "tig" with him all over the chancel, and he, unlike the other girls, was not able to run as fast as her, being nearer eighty than seventy.

Everyone gazed, fascinated by this unique incident that had so livened up the usually dull and dreary morning service. Sister Maude went white and stood by helpless, held imprisoned by her dignity; the other nuns stood uncertainly, their eyes flickering nervously between Bille's exploits and the now quivering Sister Maude. It was Miss Howkins who came to the rescue. Striding up the aisle like a modern Joan of Arc, she rectified the situation by capturing Bille, who had by now got quite tired of the game and was more than willing to be caught. She ran to Miss Howkins, laughing happily: Bille had never imagined that anyone could have so much fun in church and now realised why everyone went twice and sometimes three times every Sunday. What puzzled Bille was why the other girls appeared to dislike it so much, as she'd had an absolutely lovely time and the game had been so much fun! Poor Bille may well have thought it fun, but she was given the ultimate punishment; she was barred from church for at least two years!

Everyone was at church except for Maggie, a real Cinderella figure who had to stay at home to make the "pudding"! "Stir up Sunday" was one of the most important Sundays in the Home. A little thrill of anticipation ran through Paddy when the congregation chanted the familiar words:-

Stir up we beseech Thee the wills
Of Thy faithful people, that they
Plenteously bringing forth
Good works, made by Thee.
Be plenteously rewarded,
Through Jesus Christ our Lord,
Amen.

She shouted a fervent "Amen". She loved the way religion was interwoven into their lives and the way she could tell the passing of the year through the hymns and Collects, Epistles and Gospels they chanted day in and day out in church and chapel. The girls went to chapel twice a day and to church on Sunday and Paddy loved the rich fabric and familiar and resonant Biblical words.

The service was over and the girls returned home, but not in such an orderly manner, for though they were still in a crocodile, the pairs were spaced out in less than regimental fashion. She was with Sister Helena Mary who always stopped at the corner of Marks and Spencer to buy "The Scotsman". Sister Helena Mary was small and dainty and had a soft Cumbrian accent. Paddy fidgeted, wishing the newspaper man would hurry up. She looked at his blue fingers; it was only November, but it was very cold. "A season of mists and mellow fruitfulness", the poem said at school, but she knew that meant cold. Paddy beamed at the man, feeling ashamed at her impatience and sorry she'd willed him to hurry with fingers so cold in spite of his fingerless gloves. At last his trembling fingers had counted the change and she and Sister Helena Mary were once more on their way. They passed Canvins, the butchers, passed the kitchen shop and the jewellers. Sister Helena Mary sensed her excitement and the two sped along, Sister Helena Mary's veil was billowing behind like a ship in full sail. Paddy smiled at the Sister, pleased she would soon be home for the real event on "Stir up Sunday". At last they were turning into the long sweeping drive and had just opened the imposing front door when the gong boomed out, signalling the start of the ceremony.

All the inhabitants of the home were squeezed into the kitchen, even Miss Digby, a God-daughter of Sister Maude, who had a private room in the Sisters' wing and who worked in The Crescent, the road running beside the home: She was an austere woman who always wore tweeds, twinsets and pearls and was of indeterminate age. Miss Digby never spoke to the girls, indeed seldom venturing into the girls' part of the home, but when they came face to face and confrontation was unavoidable, she gave them a frosty, wintry smile. Miss Digby never came to their church, preferring to go to the Trinity Church, next door to the Home. Paddy wondered why they didn't go to that church too, but she did like St Paul's, even though it seemed a long way to walk. She looked round the kitchen; it was a large room, which at the moment seemed dwarfed by the crowd which gathered, summoned by the strident banging of the gong. This was one of the few times of the year when everyone, staff, nuns, girls and those like Miss Digby who were never really part of the Home usually, came together. There was no hierarchical order either and Maggie, fat and proud, was in her kingdom and her element; Cinderella was at the ball for this short hour. Paddy looked at the contents of the large bowl that Maggie, cackling merrily and triumphantly, was stirring. That was the Christmas pudding! She imagined how it would be on Christmas Day, rich, dark and steaming and standing bravely with the bright green holly crowning it.

Miss Howkins took up her traditional place, a dress rehearsal for the great day, only this time, instead of calling out the names randomly, she called them in strict chronological order, starting with the youngest and finishing with the most senior members of the community. Paddy was thrilled that this very important ceremony started with the youngest, as usually the older ones had the first, and very often the only, go at anything. She watched Bille as she made the all important wish and was disappointed she was the middle one as, if Paddy had been the youngest, she could have been the first and, she knew, she would have done it with so much more dignity. She wondered what Bille, her wicked, black snapping eyes brimful of delight, mischief and devilry, would wish for. Donna was called and as she wished, her long golden curls nearly touched the dark mixture. It was nearly Paddy's turn and she wondered if she should wish for curls, but as she'd been trying to decide since last year, she really knew what her wish was going to be.

It was her turn! Paddy made her way to the front of the crowd of girls and staff and was placed on the chair that was provided for those too small to reach the pudding. She stood on the chair, wobbling until Doreen, her favourite member of staff, put out her hand to steady her. A thrill of excitement ran through her. She grasped the large wooden spoon and closed her eyes earnestly. Paddy knew exactly what she wanted; a pink pig! She knew why she wanted it too. That summer, the girls had put on a review for the local dignitaries who supported St. Etheldreda's.. The three sisters had taken part in the review; they had put on a special performance of "I'm a little teapot". It had been hard work teaching Bille and Paddy could still remember the words:

I'm a little teapot short and stout,
Here's my handle and here's my spout.
When you call for tea up, hear me shout
Tip me up and pour me out.

Of course, in spite of all the rehearsals, Bille could not do it properly; she always tipped the wrong way or fell over altogether, but on this occasion, she had done both! Paddy glowed with pride when she thought of the laughter and the applause they'd received, but it was the big ones' play she'd been thinking of when she had decided to spend her one wish, surely a magic wish, on a pig, a pink pig. It had been a sketch about a school and Ethel had come, in crying that her pig had died last night, the one they had been saving for Christmas. Paddy had immediately thought how lovely it would be to have a pig, a fat, snub-nosed, curly tailed pink pig for Christmas. Paddy hadn't yet worked out why you should save a pig for Christmas when you had already got it, but since then it had been her dearest wish and so on "Stir up Sunday" she wished for her pig. It had not been an easy decision; Paddy was very positive she wanted the pig, but supposing she wished for it and it didn't come true? That would mean Christmas wasn't true, and there was no magic! Christmas had always been a magical time and although Paddy was small, she already knew some things are not for ever and ever: the magic goes, disappears, and you're left with a dream, never being certain if the magic was there at all. She had worried whether to wish for something smaller, less important to her, but she wanted the pig so much and could not forgo it. Paddy turned her attention back to the crowded kitchen.

Paddy looked down at the cat that was brushing past her legs and bent down to stroke her, but the cat was gone, oblivious of her desire to stroke it, and she only succeeded in annoying the girl in front as she bumped into her. She looked at the gleaming red tiles that spoke of the large amounts of "elbow grease" which had gone into them. The kitchen was one of her favourite rooms, that and the chapel. This was Maggie's domain: Maggie's throne room where Maggie, poor, fat, unloved Maggie was queen. The big blue dresser was always filled with shining pots and pans and the scrubbed white pine table was sturdy and secure, not like the table in the scullery. That table was covered with an old oilcloth and shook dangerously when you put anything on it. Paddy looked round at the Aga which was very big and very black, not a dirty black, but a dull black. It was where Maggie did all the cooking. It ate up nearly half the wall, was black, big and warm and was always smartly turned out with its coat of boot blacking. It had six hot plates and four ovens as well as six drawers to keep food hot and Paddy thought you had to feed it with coal. It was Maggie's pride and joy: only Maggie fed it and looked after it. No one else was allowed to touch it.

Paddy looked at the older girls who were now stirring the pudding, Pat, Kathleen, Ann and Dora. Dora didn't go to school, so she stayed at home to help with the housework. Dora was also fat and had a big, brown spot on her face with a big whisker on it, but she wasn't as nice as Maggie. Paddy pondered for a while; perhaps you have to be fat to stay in the Home to help? Perhaps if you were fat, then you had to stay at home wherever you lived? She wondered about this. Dora never seemed happy, as her mouth was always in a petulant scowl. Dora didn't have cats though; perhaps you needed cats or a glass eye to make you happy.

It was Doreen's turn to stir the pudding; Doreen was very beautiful with long, black, glossy hair that she wore plaited and coiled around her head like a halo. Doreen was staff, but wasn't called Miss Something, just Doreen. Paddy loved Doreen, who was Scottish: you mustn't say Scotch because that was rude, Doreen had told her. Doreen had a round face, beautiful laughing brown eyes and red cheeks; "bonny" cheeks, Doreen had said when they saw someone with the same coloured cheeks. Doreen also had a most lovely soft Scottish voice and she would sing to Paddy when they were alone, *"Speed Bonny Boat" and "You'll Take the High Road."* Doreen smiled at her and Paddy felt a thrill of pride that Doreen was her friend; she was so excited, she almost forgot to smile back and she and Doreen chuckled silently over the heads of the others in the kitchen. She did hope Doreen's wish would come true.

Miss Darnell always came in especially for "Stir Up Sunday" and always came looking very smart. Paddy looked at Miss Darnell with curiosity, noting that she had legs today. Miss Darnell was always sitting down at the sewing machine in the room next to the Laundry Room, so Paddy had never seen her with legs. She wondered what Miss Darnell wished for, but even Paddy's imagination didn't stretch that far! Now it was Miss

Howkins' turn. She liked Miss Howkins and she too had long hair; it wasn't black like Doreen's, but grey-brown and in a bun, always tied with a brown ribbon. Miss Howkins was kind too: when Paddy and Bille came to the Home, their favourite place to hide from the noise and the crowds of girls was under the school room table and only Dawn and Miss Howkins could persuade them to come out. Under the table no-one spoke to them or hurt them and there they would crouch cuddling each other like two little koala bears. They were safe there, as most people were unaware of their presence. Dawn had sat under the table with them, but as she had come to the Home nearly a year before them and had many friends, she didn't stay long. Miss Howkins would come and talk to them and on rare occasions, she would persuade them to come out to sit on her bony knee. Then Donna came and Miss Howkins no longer had time, as Miss Howkins and Donna really loved each other and spent as much time together as they could. Donna said she'd been in Miss Howkins' room and seen her with her hair down!

Now it was the turn of Sister Helena Mary, who was very small. Why was she so small? Was it because she didn't go to bed? Paddy knew you grew in bed and had been worried when Dawn went to the Isolation hospital as she was in bed all day, and Paddy thought she might grow into a giant, bigger than Father Hankey and even bigger than the Reverent Mother. Paddy turned her attention back to the kitchen and Sister Helena Mary, who was poised to make her wish. What did nuns wish for? She thought hard. They couldn't wish for pink pigs! Paddy chuckled to herself, her bright blue eyes sparkling with mischief, lighting up her rather solemn face at the thought of Sister Helena Mary with a pink pig! Her face resumed its habitual look of serious concentration as she returned to the problem in hand, namely what nuns wished for. Perhaps Sister Helena Mary wished she were bigger. Are nuns allowed to wish? They have three knots in their girdles that meant they had promised God three things: always to obey, never to have anything of their own but always be poor, and never to marry. Poverty, Obedience and Chastity, but surely that meant they couldn't wish for anything. They couldn't have a pink pig even, but could they wish to be bigger or have a glass eye? Sister Helena Mary bought "The Scotsman" every week; did that mean she sinned every week. She would have to confess it to the Reverend Mother; that was a terrible thought! But could the Reverend Mother hear her? After all, the Reverend was very tall!

Sister Maude was wishing now and she was very ugly and bristles stuck out of her chin. Perhaps she could wish she were pretty? Sister Helena Mary was pretty; why did God make some people pretty and some ugly with bristles on their chins? `Paddy thought long and hard. If God gave the nuns their bodies, surely that meant they couldn't change them? She gave up the problem; it was beyond her. Paddy looked at Sister Helena Mary; she came from near Scotland, Maryport. Perhaps it was named after her or perhaps she was named for the town? Paddy's attention was caught by Sister Maude stirring the pudding. Sister Maude was always last; she was squarish, had yellow skin and always looked cross. She looked at Sister Maud's bristles and wondered if they were as long as Michael Finnigan's, who *"had whiskers on his chinagin"*. Paddy wondered if Sister Maude's bristles grew when she slept: surely not!!

Suddenly it was all over. Sister Maude was smiling, but still looked cross. Everyone had stirred and wished; they all filed out of the kitchen, leaving a room that grew bigger and bigger as it gradually emptied of the huge crush of staff and children all going about their business. The older ones, those over seven, had to learn the collect for the day every Sunday before lunch, but Paddy didn't have to learn it yet. She could count very well; she liked numbers, as they always came out right, always told the truth. You couldn't fool with numbers and Paddy already knew two alphabets, the deaf and dumb one and the real one. She skipped along, very proud of her accomplishments; today she could do anything. She decided to sit under the table to think and as she had so much to think about, she had better start right now. Paddy made her way to the schoolroom table; it was big and strong and made of wood. She liked tables. They kept you safe. People didn't come and hurt you if you were under the table, and there were no snakes under the table. Snakes! What a silly thought! Why had she thought of snakes? Paddy had never even seen one. You could pretend anything underneath a table and no one could laugh at you. She got up quickly, banging her head. Paddy thought about it for a moment then decided to cry. Yes, she'd go and find Doreen and tell her about her sore head. Doreen would comfort her in her soft Scottish voice. Cheered at this thought, but having the presence of mind to keep the tears streaming down her face, she ran off to find Doreen.

Chapter 6: Locked Doors and Closed Shutters

Christmas was coming! It was nearly here. There was an air of mystery emanating from the Sisters' quarters. The secrecy surrounding Paddy made little shivers of delight run up and down her spine. The library door was locked and the library shutters barred and St. Andrews, the Sisters' sitting room was also locked. Paddy knew the precise moment they'd been locked and barred as all the girls did. Paddy had checked them herself, as all the girls had. She had felt a flicker of apprehension in case the doors weren't locked at all as she turned the handle gently, but this was quickly transformed into a thrill of delight as she realised, turning and pushing with all her six year old might, that the doors were well and truly locked. She had to honour the tradition of creeping through the Sisters' garden to peer through the cracks in the library shutters. It was the thing to do: it had to be done, but she was always terrified that she would actually see something. That was the magic of Christmas, Paddy thought, the secrets, but all was safe. There were other people besides Paddy who were concerned that secrets should remain secrets. She had also visited the Sewing Room, hoping without hope that Miss Darnell might have a "new" dress for her; she knew they weren't really new, but Miss Darnell just smiled at her sudden appearance in the Sewing Room. They chatted for a while and without either of them mentioning it, Paddy knew there was nothing for her….yet.

This morning Paddy had watched the big girls help to prepare for Christmas. First of all they had to fetch the special, very large key to the china cupboards: these were two big cupboards that stretched from floor to ceiling in the Refectory. Sister Maude had the key and would only relinquish it to the eldest girl and only on very special occasions like Christmas and Easter. Then the girls, again only the older ones, would squabble over who should do what jobs. This was solved in the most "democratic" way possible, the biggest, strongest and most aggressive taking the best jobs and leaving the youngest and weakest girls to continue bickering to decide who should have the worst job of all. This too was finally settled in the time honoured way to the satisfaction of everyone, except the youngest and the weakest, but they didn't count anyway. The jobs were eventually begun and operation Christmas was at last underway. Paddy had crept into the refectory, being careful to keep out of sight; experience had taught her that often little ones should not be seen or heard if they were to avoid being given the jobs no one else would do. Paddy loved the moment when one of the nuns opened the big cupboards, for although the girls fetched the key from Sister Maude, the opening of the cupboards was far too important to be trusted to them. Paddy loved the way the beautiful china gleamed at her from the dark recesses of the cupboards. The china was all the same design: a design of flamboyant exotic and fantastic birds and flowers. There were plates: dinner plates, side plates, pudding plates, soup bowls and pudding bowls. There were teacups, coffee cups, coffee saucers and tea saucers. There were teapots, coffee pots, hot water jugs and milk jugs. There were serving dishes, gravy boats and cream jugs. In fact there was everything anyone could want in the way of china and enough to serve well over forty places.

The unloading was supervised by one of the nuns and then the bigger girls would march, laden like African porters in the picture books which told about the terrible fate of the brave missionaries who went to darkest Africa to bring God into foreign lives. The girls went down two flights of stairs and onto the uneven stone floor of the scullery with its cockroaches and green wooden cupboards. They would climb on to the slatted wooden platform and then place their burdens on the right hand draining board. One of the older girls would fill the two sinks with very hot water and then one of the younger big ones would pass the pieces of china to the girl at the right hand sink, who would wash them in the hot, soapy water and then pass them to an even smaller big girl who would, after sluicing them in the hot water in her sink, place them on to the left hand draining board. One of the bigger ones would then dry them and give them to the biggest girls, who would put them away in the green scullery cupboards ready for the big day. Paddy never looked in the green cupboards at the china; they never seemed as grand as the great, dark, polished cupboards in the Refectory.

After the completion of this job, they were ready to start the next one, the one that really heralded the rapid approach of Christmas: within days the celebration of the birth of the Christ Child would be upon them. It was time to decorate the Refectory and the Chapel Hall. The Chapel Hall was adjacent to the Refectory and over both, hovering like Gabriel himself, was the Chapel, watching, guarding, and ordering the life of the community. The decorations were simple paper chains that the younger ones had made. Paddy had helped make them too, just as she had helped gather the walnuts for the pudding when they fell from the enormous tree in the autumn. The decorations were more special, as, after all, you couldn't tell if the walnuts in your slice of pudding were the same ones you had collected, but the decorations were different. As she watched the big ones put them up, she could see exactly which ones she had made, as she had done them in a special order. Paddy hadn't marked them in any way, for that would have merited a punishment, but she had arranged the colours in a special pattern. She loved order and precise patterns and the beauty of the paper chains was that she could recognise them as hers.

Paddy was pleased and very proud that she'd had that idea. They were hers, but only she knew it and, as she was the only one to know it, they couldn't be taken away from her. She had learnt from bitter experience that as long as she didn't claim things out loud, but just knew in her heart they were hers, then they remained hers; nobody could take them away. If however, she said something was hers and someone said it wasn't, Paddy either had to fight for it, and she wasn't very good at fighting, or she had to disclaim it. Using this system, she "owned" lots of things. She had her "own" pew in chapel, her "own" hymn, her "own" psalm, her "own" collect, and her "own" song at school; they were all hers and they would always be hers. Paddy graciously allowed others to claim her hymn as theirs, allowed them to sit on her chair and pew, but they remained hers. She was pleased others were getting pleasure out of using her things, but they remained hers. Paddy loved the crib, especially the young shepherd boy with the lamb. Her shepherd boy had been placed in the best place to see the Christ child. Paddy had "allowed" someone else to place him there so he would get the best place and he smiled at her in gratitude for her kindness, when no one else was looking.

The Chapel was quiet and the peace enveloped her. Everyone had gone, but Paddy was still kneeling with her eyes fixed on the crib. Only she sat in the still silent world, gazing at the age-old story in pageant before her. She stared at the tableaux and her thoughts drifted to wreaths of incense as they were released into the lime trees lining The Crescent and then up into the freedom of the clouds above. Paddy's big, blue eyes drank in the colour and splendour of the altar cloth and her senses swam in the heady perfume of candles and the oil which burned continuously to show that the "Host" was always there in the special casket on the wall. Sister Eleanor said that "The Holy Ghost" lived in the casket, but Paddy knew He didn't because He lived in church. Sister Eleanor was a nun and she was supposed to be cleverer than all the other nuns, but Paddy knew more than Sister Eleanor. She supposed it was because Sister Eleanor was old and couldn't remember. Paddy, alone of all the girls, came here when the nuns were at Vespers; she just sat and let the sweet voices wash over her. The beautiful words flowed over her and through her, releasing her mind in a way that was not possible in the midst of the hustle and bustle of the Home . The nuns marvelled at one so young being so pious and thought she'd been called by God to be a missionary when she was older, but Paddy came for the freedom it allowed her thoughts and the inner peace and serenity she received.

Christmas is coming! The rhyme insinuated itself into her head:

> *Christmas is coming,*
> *The geese are getting fat.*
> *Please put a penny in the old man's hat.....*

That was the newspaperman on the corner by Marks and Spencer, his fingers blue with cold and his smile as warm as a summer's day. Christmas is coming, Christmas is coming! Christmas was the best festival of all. Paddy remembered last Christmas; most of the girls had gone to a big party given by the Canadian Air force; she had forgotten that. The men gave all of the girls a big present each; she and her sisters couldn't understand why they had the best presents, as usually the girls with mums and dads received the extra presents. The sisters were allowed to hold the dolls until they left the party and then they had been taken away and put? Yes, that was it; the dolls were put in the big chest on the Sisters' landing, only to be played with on very special occasions. There had only been one special occasion she could remember, and then she couldn't think why it was considered special: she and Bille and Dawn had played with the dolls one afternoon on the floor of the sisters' landing. They'd had a lovely time, but after a very short time they'd had to return the huge dolls, with their long golden hair and smiling faces, to their dark, coffin-like chest, only emerging to laughter and light at another special occasion, just like Sister Evelyn, Paddy thought, who was only brought out on special occasions.. The dolls had beautiful clothes, fine underwear and even smart shoes, yet they lay in their chest, unthought of and unloved except for the rare times they were taken out and made a fuss of. Christmas was like that; decorations only made their all too brief annual appearance, but the poor dolls didn't even have a regular special time to be taken out.

Christmas was coming! She thought of the church by the market square that would be resplendent with a majestic tree and thousands of candles. The candles would glow and glitter making Paddy feel she was in Cinderella's castle, sparkling with crystal. It was difficult to realise that the sparkling silver streamers on the tree were just decorations, yet she knew they were and, despite the fairy-tale sight, despite the tawdry tinsel, the stark dark, green of the tree itself would compel the eye to look at it through the glitter that surrounded it. The tree was uprooted and dying, yet it was to this that the eye was drawn again and again.

She thought of the screen that separated the nave from the chancel; it too would be aglitter with tinsel interwoven with holly and ivy, and yet far above, dominating the scene, causing all eyes to turn, stood the wooden crucifix. It, like the tree, would be surrounded with all the transient joyfulness of Christmas and the brief, shining hope it proclaimed to the human race, and yet it was to the plain wooden unadorned figure of Jesus that eyes were drawn to again and again. Paddy's eyes lit up and her heart sang as she remembered the gaiety of the Christmas scenes, but she knew the feeling would not last: like the dolls, it should and did bring pleasure and joy and was looked forward to because it brightened up her dull, drab institutionalised world, but the real joy was to be found in the enduring quality of the figure on the cross. There bespoke the real message, that even when their gifts were taken away on Boxing Day, and in spite of all the bad things, Christmas would come again. There would be glitter and fairy-tale castles, but most of all there would be the cross symbolising hope.

There was a sound! She jerked her thoughts back to the silent chapel and listened intently. Was someone coming? No, the footsteps died away. Paddy was back in the world of reality; she felt stiff. She relaxed on the floor once more. Suddenly a loud bell pierced the silence and brought her once more back to reality; it was the bell for dinner and she hadn't finished her job yet. Paddy seemed to have been in the chapel for hours, so she sighed and resolutely went downstairs to face the clamour, which was life in the Home.

It was time for bed. The afternoon had dragged by on leaden feet even though she'd been busy doing the work she hadn't done in the morning. Paddy had her bath and hung up her sock for Father Christmas and made the usual firm resolution to stay awake until Father Christmas came and then climbed into bed and fell instantly asleep. It was a dreamless sleep, a peaceful sleep; a sleep unpunctuated by the horrendous night noises, by Maggie's strident cry in the dark, moonlit garden or by Joyce's slip slopping sleepwalks. Paddy woke much later to the sound of a door softly closing. She was not afraid. The night was silent and she delighted in the silence, revelled in it. She lay for a few minutes, drinking in the peace and serenity and allowed the quiet joy of the moment to wash over her. She surrendered her mind and body to the peace of the night and in turn it enveloped her, quieting her questioning. It was not to last, this curious acquiescence, for suddenly Paddy remembered and her thin body gave a little jump of excitement, pushing aside the peace and serenity that had been hers a few short minutes ago.

It was Christmas! Had HE been? Paddy listened intently. There was no sound to disturb the peace of the Christmas night. She was safe. She carefully pushed the bedclothes back and quietly edged her way down the bed, pausing every few moments to listen in case she should be discovered, but still no sound broke the silence. Paddy felt that something was missing in the darkness, but couldn't think what it could be. She sat hunched on the bed thinking. Suddenly in the peace and quiet it came to her: the nightmare noises had gone, obliterated by the halcyon joy of Christmas. She gave a little squirm of true delight. Paddy knew from the bitter experience of earlier years, when she and her sisters had slept peacefully downstairs, that the noises would be back tomorrow, but that did not mar her happiness; tonight they were gone. Tonight she was free

Paddy continued her journey to the bottom of the bed, and could scarcely contain her cry of ecstasy as her trembling fingers encountered the bulging sock. The night was pitch black and she was suddenly afraid to feel for her pink pig. If he came at all, he'd come like this, but now the moment had come, she was assailed with doubts. Paddy remembered, in despair, how she had wished so often for all sorts of things, and really believed they would come and yet…She remembered a bible reading she'd once heard that said she could move mountains if she had faith; well she'd had faith and the intensity of that faith had closed her eyes to reality, so when she had opened them once more, everything was as it always had been. Paddy remembered the times she had closed her eyes and ears to the night noises, had been certain if she could just count to ten, twenty, a hundred even, then they would go away, but they hadn't. She had believed it, really believed it, but….Paddy wished she had never asked for pig; she had broken one of her own rules, never to ask for anything so you can never be disappointed. She had discovered early in life that living was possible if you had no hopes; if you never expected anything or hoped for anything, then you never reached the depths of despair. The "Slough of Despair" was there and it was reached by the road of expectancy.

Paddy sat on the edge of the bed, big silent tears rolling down her face. What was she to do? If she didn't look, if she obeyed the rule: "no looking till morning", perhaps pig would be there in the morning. The logic of this appealed to her, she liked it. But the night was so peaceful, so very peaceful that surely if a wish was to come true, it would be tonight. The night seemed to be a magic night and her pig should be magical. Paddy was pondering the problem as only a small child could, when she suddenly remembered the story of Abraham and Isaac; Abraham had to prove his faith, may be she should do the same. Trembling, she shut her eyes and stretched out her hand. Nothing! Paddy leaned further towards the end of the bed and her fingers encountered something warm and soft. She knew instantly what it was; she couldn't see it, but she knew. She was silently crying with happiness. She clasped pig tightly to her skinny chest and almost danced back to bed. Paddy knew more happiness than she thought she had known in the whole of her young life. Nothing so wonderful had ever happened to her before; her whole body trembled with delight. She longed for someone to share it with, but with knowledge too old for her years, born of that hard taskmaster, experience, she also knew that true happiness could seldom be shared. Something was lost in the telling, and as so often happened, the knowledge was often debased, ridiculed, scorned or ignored. Instantly, the happiness was gone, obliterated as if it had never been there in the first place, leaving the void that constantly reminded her of her foolishness. Paddy slept as soon as her head touched the pillow and walked through acres of gardens with her pink pig. Music played and there were snowdrops and wallflowers and honeysuckle and her pink pig.

Chapter 7: And Christ Is Born

Paddy awoke to an unfamiliar buzz; normally the morning sounds were subdued. The girls would speak in whispers, as if they somehow knew, as she did, of the night noises and were ashamed of their fears in the brightness of morning. Today on this special day, there was a delicious buzz, rather like a very fat, happy bumblebee visiting his favourite flower. Paddy opened her eyes. She never opened her eyes until she had listened first, as she knew how important it was to prepare herself for the events the day might bring. After sleep, you were always unprepared for the sheer drudgery of routine, and the awful loneliness you felt inside. She had to listen and remind herself each morning and prepare for the day ahead: that way the hurts of the day could be minimised.

Today was different though; today there was a buzz. Paddy saw, when she opened her eyes, she was late. But today the discovery did not fill her with alarm. All the girls were up, their "stockings" opened and surprises strewn across the beds. There was a sweet smell of oranges around the dormitory and the excited traffic of clattering footsteps as the girls ran up and down the long corridors, comparing the trifles they'd got in their long grey socks. Paddy's arm ached. She pondered over the cause of this discomfort, and the answer hit her, bringing with it once more, sheer delight. Her pink pig! She gasped; he was very pink, very fat and his two bright bootblack eyes gazed into her bright blue ones. Paddy hugged him fiercely and wondered if he would mind lying down, so she could look in her sock to see what else she had been given. She put him down gently, experimentally and looked at him carefully. He smiled lazily, his pig eyes twinkling, and with a sense of expectancy, she turned to her sock.

Immediately the girls gathered round and Paddy felt part of them, secure in the attention she was being paid, attention she wanted and needed. She pulled the objects out, one by one. A bar of soap, some marbles, a tiny pack of playing cards, a silver threepenny bit and in the toe, an orange. So intent had she been, she hadn't noticed the girls gradually moving away and it wasn't until the breakfast gong reverberated through the large house, that she realised how late she was. Paddy panicked. She wasn't ready! She was late! She was late again! She hastily ran down the stairs and along the corridor into the washroom, gave herself "a lick and a promise" and hurried back through the corridor and back up the stairs. It wasn't so easy going back, as she was against the tide of traffic caused by the rest of the girls rushing down the stairs in answer to the gong's summons. She reached her dormitory once more, flung on her clothes, whisked back her bed covers and then spent several precious moments wondering what to do with Pig. Paddy decided to let him sleep late, so tucking him into bed, she once more dashed downstairs, both flights this time, flew through the hall, chapel corridor, past the nursery and into the chapel hall. She was late as usual, but peering round the Refectory door, she was relieved to see not everyone was seated.

Paddy entered the Refectory and gazed in wonder at a sight that, though she had seen it three times before, always filled her with delight. The Christmas decorations were mingling with the traditional holly, ivy and other evergreen garlands and filled the whole room with colour. Her paper chains were there too and she felt a tremor of pride as she observed them. Paddy had forgotten them in her worry and delight over pig; she was pleased she had forgotten, as the vista before her hit her with greater force, causing her to stand still, staring at the colours, her skinny body hunched up with excitement and her blue eyes wide in wonderment. Dimly through the furore, she heard voices telling her to hurry up. Paddy knew she had to find her place name so she would know where to sit. She looked round, hoping to see a spare place which would save her the long task of reading all the name tags, but there appeared to be no vacant chairs at all; every seat seemed to be filled. What should she do? Everyone was staring at her. Suddenly Miss Howkins' face loomed out of the mists of indecision and Paddy saw Miss Howkins' finger pointing; she smiled gratefully and hurried in the direction the finger pointed. She saw, as if in a dream, an empty seat next to Doreen. She could scarcely read the card by the plate; supposing it wasn't hers? Supposing someone else was late! Supposing that person should be sitting by Doreen? But Doreen was smiling at her. She looked at the name: it was hers! Tears of happiness sprung to her eyes and she clutched Doreen's hand as everyone stood up to say grace.

Everyone sat down and Paddy gazed at the beautiful china. She traced with her finger the exotic and flamboyant shape of the birds and listened while Doreen tried to answer her more difficult questions in her soft, lilting Scottish voice. They always had the special breakfast, every Christmas. It was traditional. She liked traditions; they were warm, safe things. No matter what happened, there would always be the Christmas breakfast of ham, lean ham, not the fatty and gristly ham they sometimes had for dinner, rolls, not the stale bread they usually had, butter and marmalade and they would eat off the "Bird" china. Paddy beamed at everyone and thought how lucky the plates were to only see smiling faces and hear happy voices. She whispered to Doreen the news about pig. She hadn't told anyone else. Paddy had been determined to tell Doreen the good news first. She hadn't imagined she would be able to tell her so soon. It was frustrating that although they lived in the same house, sometimes Paddy could be searching for Doreen all morning, only to be eventually told that she had gone out! Doreen's round face lit up and she squeezed Paddy's hand under the table, and the rest of breakfast passed as in a dream. Paddy shyly asked Doreen if she would like to meet Pig and when Doreen said she would be delighted, Paddy's joy knew no bounds.

There was no chapel or toilet duty that day, so straight after breakfast Paddy took Doreen by the hand, climbed the two flights of stairs and introduced her to Pig. Doreen admired his boot-button eyes, his roundness and his vivid colour and after the formalities had been observed, she and Doreen planned his day. Doreen suggested that due to all the excitement and bustle, it might be better if Pig were to stay in bed; Paddy could come and keep him company at times during the day. Paddy thought this an excellent idea. The gong rang out, signalling they were to get ready for church. She liked the gong better than the bell; it was a large golden gong with a stick that had a large leather covered ball at the end. You used this to hit the gong and you had to hit it in the centre for the best sound. It was the Sisters' gong and was only used for the whole house on Sundays and church festivals when the household, staff, nuns and girls, ate together. For common days the girls had just a hand bell; it was also a golden colour, but it did not ring as loudly as the gong and the sound it made was raucous compared with the clear, pure mellow ring of the gong.

Doreen had gone and Paddy was on her own. She looked at Pig and, whilst agreeing that Pig should stay in bed, she knew she couldn't leave him there on his own. She pushed him underneath her jumper and ran downstairs to the Tube, where their coats were. Paddy put her coat on carefully and went to Miss Howkins to have her hair brushed. Bille was there, having her hair brushed, so she would have to wait. Bille's blue-black hair was tangled again and Bille would twist and turn to avoid her hair being brushed, grumbling and shrieking all the while. Bille's coiffure was always a battle, but Miss Howkins was a tried and tested campaigner, a veteran of these skirmishes who always triumphed in the end. Paddy put on her shoes and, noting that the battle was nearly over, with another clear victory for Miss Howkins, presented herself to have her hair brushed before flying upstairs to join the back of the crocodile. She carefully positioned herself so that her partner was the other side to Pig and then held her breath while Sister Helena Mary checked them. The nod came and they were outside in the crisp, cold air that cut through their dull regulated lives, bringing with it the clarity and purity that only the natural world has.

There was no snow, no snowdrops, but it was a beautiful day. It was special because of the absence of snow and snowdrops. If they had been there, her eyes may not have noticed the less showy beauty that was all around. The frost sparkled like diamonds and edged the last autumn leaves with silver; snow, though beautiful, would have obliterated them, but the frost enhanced them, bringing them to life in a last burst of defiant colour. There were fewer coloured leaves and the colours were less bright than in autumn, but the red leaves of the Virginia creeper that clung to the walls of the Home still held a hint of bonfires and chestnuts. There were hundreds of spiders' webs dressed in their Christmas best of Brussels lace, edged and decorated with crystal drops. She imagined the tiny spiders spinning their webs through the night and, when the sun rose, seeing the transformation. They must have felt like Cinderella did when she was able to go to the ball. It was even more fantastic when you realised this was not a fairy story, but something that happened many times during a cold spell. The cold air stung her face, but the pale wintry sunshine illuminated the town, giving it a magical, iridescent look.

They arrived at the church and Paddy gasped as she glimpsed the interior through the big, heavy, wooden doors. The church was breathtakingly beautiful. There was a shimmering glow over the whole church, a glow that emanated from hundreds of candles on the windowsills and ledges that proliferated in every nook and cranny of the huge church. Besides the candles, there were numerous varieties of evergreen: holly, ivy, spruce and the lovely translucent Christmas rose. She had been the only one in the Home to know what it was when they were shown a picture of it in chapel and now it had a special place in her memory garden along with wallflowers, snowdrops and honeysuckle. She wondered how she knew about the Christmas rose, for she couldn't remember ever seeing one before......Paddy turned her mind back to the church, to the huge red ribbons adorning the sills, and remembered the questions she had asked Doreen about the predominant Christmas colours, dark green, red and white. She felt they were special Christmas colours and she and Doreen worked them out together: the red for the blood shed by Jesus, the white for the Star of Bethlehem and the dark green for the sprigs of young leaves on the wood of the manger and the cross, symbolising the birth of the Christ-child. Beautiful though all this was, Paddy's eyes were drawn to the tree. It was taller than she could remember or even thought possible, and the sweet smell of pine needles and incense mingled with the pungent smell of the candles to give a mystical perfume that could only be present at Christmas and therefore belonged wholly to this festival. The red and white of the choristers' robes and the brilliance of the priest's cope contrasted with the sombre, grey, stone pillars and Paddy was at one with Christmas. The familiar scene, the expected, though unimaginable beauty, brought tears to her eyes and she lived once more.

Paddy had known it would be like this, but she could never recall absolutely and exactly the effect it would have on her. She could sense the pillars would endure: they were the church. The tree would die, the tinsel would tarnish, the baubles break, but the pillars proclaimed with the cross that Christmas would come again, the real Christmas. Presents would be stolen, taken, broken or lost, but no one could take this Christmas, this feeling away; this was one thing Paddy would always remember. The sweet voices of the choirboys pierced the perfumed air and she felt she would remember this day forever. She sat in her pew, her "favourite" pew, and after gravely inspecting her neighbour and those immediately to the front and back of her, brought out Pig from where he'd been hiding. Paddy knew he couldn't understand the treasures of Christmas, but she wanted to share it with someone, or something, someone or something who would not destroy her happiness by a scathing remark or even ridicule, someone who could not take it away as it had been taken away so many times. Pig stared about him in wonderment and she hugged him tightly and let the music, lights and the beautiful familiar words wash over her and she was completely happy.

Paddy was still clutching Pig when she walked home with Sister Dorothy. Sister Dorothy didn't mention Pig, though Paddy knew Sister Dorothy had seen him. It was a sin to take Pig to church and she knew it was Sister Dorothy's duty to tell her this. She knew all about duty and the problems it caused. She knew it was her duty to be grateful for everything done for her; she knew it was her duty to pray first thing in the morning, then again later in the morning at chapel and also in the evening service in the chapel, and again last thing at night. Duty was what you had to do, something you had to do inside as well as outside; you had to feel duty as well as demonstrate it; It was rather like the lines that Sister Maude and Father Hankey quoted: *an outward and visible sign of an inward and spiritual grace.* That was duty: the quote actually referred to the Virtues, but it could have been duty. Why didn't Sister Dorothy tell her about Pig and possibly punish her too? Paddy pondered on this problem: perhaps duty didn't happen at Christmas, but people still prayed; perhaps people really changed at Christmas, and maybe that was why the night noises hadn't been there last night.

Father Hankey said people changed at Christmas. That was when he was in the pulpit, the big throne high up where he talked every Sunday. Sister Dorothy's actions proved it. Paddy thought about this; she knew some things Father Hankey said were not true, such as what people did in their homes, but this was true. Sister Dorothy had changed! She smiled at Sister Dorothy and was amazed at the lovely smile that transformed Sister Dorothy's face. She slipped her hand into Sister Dorothy's and asked if she would like to meet Pig. Paddy introduced pig and the two rather incongruous figures, the rather shabbily dressed little girl and the tall gaunt nun in black, talking animatedly, walked through the town, eventually reaching home.

Chapter 8: Traditional Times

It was lunchtime when they arrived. Paddy just had time to put Pig to bed once more, and slip down to the chapel hall before the gong sounded. She wasn't late this time, so she had plenty of time to find her seat. She found it quickly; it was next to Miss Howkins. She liked Miss Howkins because she only gave Paddy little portions that she could eat in the allotted time. They pulled crackers and Miss Howkins helped her because she couldn't get them to "crack". Paddy liked the riddles in them and everyone wore a paper hat. Sister Maude looked really funny in hers and everyone was laughing and very happy. They always had the same traditional dinner: turkey with stuffing, roast potatoes, and Brussels sprouts. Paddy liked this dinner, as it was easy to eat. The high spot of Christmas' dinner was always the pudding, the same pudding they'd stirred on "Stir up Sunday". Maggie always carried it in to much cheering and laughing; Maggie was pink with excitement and pride, her smile stretching across her face until it was wider than the Cheshire cat in "Alice in Wonderland". This was the cue for Miss Howkins to take her place behind Sister Maude's chair, but with her back to the company. "It" was about to begin!

Miss Howkins called everyone's name out at random while Sister Maude cut the pudding. It wasn't in order, so Sister Maude could not know which portion of pudding was to go to which person. This was very important because there was treasure in the form of money, hidden in the pudding, lots of silver threepenny pieces, some sixpences and just one shilling. Paddy waited with bated breath until her name was called. When she received her portion of pudding, she didn't scramble through the pudding looking for the money, as most of the girls did, but played a little game with it. On the fifth mouthful, she "might" find the money and so on. Sometimes she had to cheat a little to make it come right, but the pleasure of anticipation, of "accidentally" finding the money exactly when she predicted was enormous. Of course sometimes she didn't find anything, but these times were few and far between, for it was rare for anyone not to find something. Today Paddy was lucky, as she found two threepennies and one sixpence, too many for her system, but she didn't mind that, as finding two coins in consecutive mouthfuls was something to boast about. Miss Howkins was lucky, as she always found the shilling piece. In fact Paddy worried that one year Miss Howkins might not find it, but it was always all right. A bowl was sent round and you had to put your money into it for the poor people who didn't have any warm clothes or good food. Sister Maude said you didn't have to put your money in the bowl, but everyone did especially as Sister Maud's eyes followed the bowl and if someone was hesitating then she stared hard at them until they "willingly" put the money in the bowl! After dinner was the inevitable washing up, but today she didn't have a job, as only the big ones were allowed to touch the beautiful china, so she went up to see Pig.

Pig was where she'd left him. Paddy picked him up and told him all about the Christmas dinner and promised she would take him down at the magical time of 3:30pm. This was after the King's speech, which the staff and Sisters listened to with rapt attention every year. Paddy always thought the King timed it deliberately in order to make them wait a little while longer, but at last the gong sounded, signalling the speech was at an end. She decided to tell Pig about the King. Paddy wondered if they have kings in the pig family, but that would be silly; after all, where would the King wear his crown? She pondered whether her king wore his crown all the time. Where did he hang it up at night? Did it ever fall off? Would that be bad luck or a bad omen? Paddy had only learnt that word last week and she liked the word: "omen", like "amen", but nicer, and it didn't mean anything like "amen". It was funny how one little letter made all the difference to a word.

The speech had ended and the washing up was done and all was ready. She picked up Pig and dashed down the stairs to the small landing, down another flight of stairs, along a corridor and into the front hall, the Sisters' hall. The queue outside the library door resembled a large crowd, rather than the orderly queue the girls normally had to make. The girls at the front were listening carefully, their ears pressed closely to the door; it wasn't locked, but there was a slight reluctance, a tantalising suspense. "Try the door," came a command from the back and immediately that cry caught the attention of the gaggle of girls at the front. The handle was turned and the door offered no opposition. Every year the girls thought they hadn't put enough pressure on the door to open it, that in fact no human hand had in fact opened it. That was the magic of Christmas!

The girls, after the first initial reluctance, surged in; Paddy, as usual was at the back, but that was part of the pleasure. She liked putting off treats until the last possible moment. She went in slowly, catching her breath at the transformation. Silver, sparkling and twinkling decorations were everywhere and they swayed and swung and made a soft tinkling music in the slight draught that entered through the large white shutters that lined both full length windows and hid the wintry back garden. The coal fire glowed with a life of its own and threw strange facets of light onto the decorations and imbued the white ceiling with a kind of magical Aurora Borealis which continually changed with the light from the fire and the dancing decorations. The heavenly lights made a direct contrast to the forbidding, heavy walls of books that stared in stolid disapproval at the frivolity of the tree. The tree was swathed in tinsel and sparkled under its weight of baubles and lights. It was quite different from the tree in the church. This was a "happy tree". "Her" birds were there with their blue and rose bodies and their soft swishy tails. The fairy was almost at the top, but at the very top was the star reminding the girls of the true meaning of Christmas. Paddy studied the tree, looking for and noting the different positions of all her old favourites.

There were presents too under the tree; so many presents she wouldn't be able to count them all. Paddy and her two sisters would have one, or sometimes they were lucky and they would get two. Some of the girls would have many more, but they had mothers and fathers and therefore deserved more, as it said in the Bible: *The sins of the fathers will be visited on the children.* She'd asked Sister Dorothy what that meant, as she didn't know what a sin was, and then Sister Dorothy explained, so she knew what wicked people her parents had been. It was a funny thing, she thought, that when you had little, you received less. Paddy cuddled Pig and explained to him about the presents and then she introduced him to her favourite birds and showed him the capricious and aloof fairy and the wonder of the bright star at the top of the tree.

Suddenly Paddy was aware of the girls near her pushing her and calling her name and Father Christmas, who always came through the French windows and bizarrely through the shutters as well, was calling her name as well. It was her turn to go up and receive a present from the tree. She stumbled over the legs of the seated girls who were crowded round the tree as she tried to hurry for her present. Paddy went quickly back to Pig to show him her spoils: it was a book, "Grimm's Fairy Stories" How lovely, she really treasured books. Paddy settled down to read to Pig. Then she was called again: this time it was soap. Knowing that this was her last, she settled down contentedly to read to Pig once more. Paddy knew the soap and the book wouldn't be hers for long, that by tomorrow they would disappear as though they had never been, taken, broken or stolen. Even Pig would be gone by tomorrow morning, but that didn't matter, as today, at this minute, she had them all and no one could take away the magic of Christmas: it might not last, but there would always be another Christmas next year.

There was movement all round her, which woke her once more from her reveries: it was teatime, a special tea of sandwiches and a slice of rich and sticky Christmas cake. Tea ended and then they played a few traditional games. Paddy liked "Squeak Piggy Squeak" as Sister Maud's idea of a pig's squeak defied logic!!They also played, "How Green You Are" and Paddy wasn't sure she liked being "it"; she knew that the louder the chant, the nearer you were to the hiding place, but she worried that she would be too slow. They also played "Musical Chairs" with Sister Eleanor playing the piano. Bed came after the games without protest from anyone. Tucked up with Pig and no night noises, Paddy slept and was swept off into a magical world of twinkling lights and swishy tailed birds and Pig. Tomorrow he would be gone and she would be back to the dull, interminable routine greyness of everyday life, but no one could take away this wonderful day; it would be hers forever.

Chapter 9: A New Beginning

The summer holiday came and went; Paddy liked the long summer holiday. Many of the girls went away to spend some time with their mothers and/or fathers, so the Home was less crowded and the Sisters and staff seemed to have more time for the remaining girls and things that they couldn't usually have, such as pens, pencils and paper, seemed to be easier to borrow. Paddy liked playing "patience", but packs of cards were rarely available, even with the more relaxed regime. However, with fewer girls about, you had a better chance of keeping them until you had finished, as usually the cards would be taken from you by other girls, and this meant that when the member of staff who had found them for you asked their whereabouts, you had to confess that you had lost them, which ensured that next time it would be more difficult to get any.

There were fewer than half the girls at the home this summer and Paddy felt somehow freer; she was able to avoid most of the ritual bullying, and even Sister Maude softened and on rare occasions gave the remaining girls permission to go into the Sisters' garden where they did handstands, somersaults, "crab-walking" and other gymnastics. Paddy joined in, but she always had more trouble doing them than the other girls. Her back didn't seem to bend very easily and there were some things she couldn't do at all such as back flips. However, she was so competitive, that the gymnastics she could perform were done better than anyone else with the exception of her older sister Dawn. Paddy held the record for "walking" on her hands and doing the "crab" walk for the longest distance. Indeed there were many reasons for rejoicing during the holiday. She didn't even mind the extra work, cleaning and laying the refectory tables for lunch and washing up and clearing away as well as with fewer people there weren't so many tables.

Paddy loved going into the Sisters' garden where there were flowers, a proper lawn, a rockery and even a fig tree, which bore real figs. When the Bible reading mentioned a fig tree, she glimpsed the sense of timelessness almost woven like a "seamless garment" from those distant times to the here and now. The garden also had a walnut tree that every autumn rained walnuts and Sister Maude would promise to give the girls a penny for twenty five good walnuts. Paddy thought she must have found hundreds, but somehow the pennies never materialised. She remembered some of the older girls singing a sad song about a girl who'd sat underneath a walnut tree and had eventually died; they'd sung that to the dignitaries, Lord Luke, the lord lieutenant of the County, the Honourable Romula Russell and other worthy people, when she and her sisters had performed, "I'm a Little Teapot".

The girls, too, had their garden, but there were no flowers, just a few apple trees that never had any apples. The one by the wall belonging to Mr Piper, who owned the paper shop across the road and wouldn't let children into his shop; it became her sanctuary where in the long warm days she could sit amongst its branches and dream or read, or do a little of both. There was also a long, lavender hedge that buzzed all summer long. Many of the girls treated the lavender hedge with great respect, as there was a steady procession to the laundry and Maggie's "bluebag" was brought out again and again to help relieve the pain of the numerous bee stings. Paddy loved the hedge; every day she would go out into the garden, studying the bees and marvelling that the bees' "wellie boots" could hold so much nectar. She also counted the bees, astounded that there were so many and she knew when the long summer days were coming to an end as the bee count started falling.

Paddy liked the gardener, Tom, and she plied him with so many questions that sometimes he had to tell her, he must "ger on with me jobs", but Paddy didn't mind, she just waited for the next opportunity. Tom regularly got stung, but he always said, "It be good for me rheumatism". However, one very hot summer morning, poor Tom had no less than thirteen bee stings and had to go home. This was a record and she was curious as to where exactly the bee stings were; she asked him to show her, but all he said was, "ger on withee". Bille also liked going into the garden, but for a very different reason: she loved a challenge, so used to run round the lavender hedge six times, making sure that as many girls as possible witnessed this amazing feat. As Bille couldn't run very fast on her six year old legs, it was quite a marvellous performance and as time would tell, it was very dangerous since Bille was later diagnosed as being fatally allergic to both bee and wasp stings. Bille also, after she had amassed an audience, would take an earwig from the hole in the laburnum tree by the swing and run round the garden, shrieking with the pain as the earwig supposedly pinched her. Paddy was extremely sceptical about this feat as once she had been near the tree when Bille had finished her run and the earwig she put back in the hole looked suspiciously inert!

The summer holiday dozed by and the girls who had gone away for the summer returned to the Home in dribs and drabs, with tales of seaside and picnics, buckets and spades, films and ice-cream, though what ice-cream was, and what one did with a bucket or spade besides working in the garden, Paddy really didn't know. She'd seen pictures of the seaside in books and conceded it had looked like fun, but all in all, she thought, she preferred to stay at the Home, and hear Dawn sing to her before she went to sleep. Dawn had a lovely voice and would sing all her favourites:

Eternal Father, strong to save
Whose arm doth bind the restless wave.

She imagined the sailors in the midst of a storm crying aloud to God while the thunder roared and the lightning lit up the sky to illuminate the dreadful waves.

Another favourite was:

Dear Lord and Father of mankind
Forgive our foolish ways.

If Dawn was tired and she couldn't sing too long, Paddy always asked her to sing just the one verse:

> *Drop thy still dews of quietness*
> *Till all our strivings cease.*
> *Take from our souls the strain and stress,*
> *Until our ordered lives confess*
> *The beauty of thy peace*

When the night noises came, Paddy would keep saying over and over, *the beauty of thy peace*, but even that didn't work. She couldn't understand how at one time the dormitory would be filled with beauty and silence, except for Dawn's lovely sweet voice, but only hours later everyone would be unhappy, and the room was filled with pain.

During this long holiday, Paddy felt she was being "told off" more than usual; it was "Paddy do this…" or "Paddy don't do that…." Apparently the nuns had seen her visiting the chapel where she either read in peace and solitude or just listened to the lime trees whispering to her on the avenue outside and they had decided that she was praying and therefore was being called by God to be a missionary. They often finished their reprimands with, "You will never be a missionary if you do this or that." Paddy really did not like the idea of being a missionary as she had seen pictures where missionaries had been burnt on a huge fire, thrown over cliffs or stabbed to death; usually the people doing the killing were men with skirts on and nothing else. Paddy was usually slow to take offence and indeed she took little notice of the "real" world about her, but whether it was because there were fewer girls and she could not "hide" so effectively, or the staff were not so busy and therefore they noticed more, she was feeling very piqued and it was becoming quite a problem, but as there seemed no real solution, she turned her mind to other things. However the problem was solved in an unexpected way.

Summer was chased away by the autumn wind, and Paddy was now in the "big" school, so she didn't have to walk quite so far. She loved school so the "big" school held no terrors for her, but she found her teacher difficult, as unlike Miss Daniels who smiled with her face, not her eyes, Miss Fyres did not smile at all! Paddy enjoyed the work and especially loved the times when they could choose a book for Miss Fyres to read, but actively disliked a precocious boy, Brian Merrill who always shouted out, "Can we have "Brer Rabbit again?" and so for most of the time, Brer Rabbit was stuck once more in the briar patch, and once more and again once more… Poor Brian also irritated Paddy, as whenever they'd had a holiday from school and their teacher asked who had gone away, or who had some news to tell the rest of the class, Brian always shouted out that, once again, he'd gone to Billing Aquadrome and once again, and again once more. She almost wished he'd stayed there! Paddy wasn't cross that he had somewhere to go, rather that he would shout so loudly that their teacher always asked him what he had done, and as he seemed to do the same thing every time, she couldn't learn anything new.

October came and went in strips of "old man's beard" and tiny, hard, red- green blackberries on the nature table. Miss Fyres encouraged her class to bring items for the nature table, but although the Home girls went for a walk Saturday and Sunday afternoons, there was little chance of seeing or gathering anything for the table when they were confined to a crocodile. It was a Friday afternoon when Paddy opened the "little" front door to catch up with the crocodile walking to afternoon school, and noticed Dilly was on the Sisters' steps talking to Sister Maude; it was unusual because the crocodile could just be seen disappearing round the corner. She went over to where they were talking and soon discovered that when Dilly had stayed with her mother in the summer, her mother had changed her name. It made no difference to Dilly, as Sister Maud had always called her Dilly and she would always be called that in the Home, although it wasn't the name her mother called her and it certainly wasn't the name she was christened with. Dilly, Sister Maude had decided, was the name that most suited her. What was strange was that Sister Maude didn't change anyone else's name. Paddy tentatively asked whether she had a second name and was very surprised and delighted when she was told she had: it was Marlene. Paddy was deep in thought over the weekend; she believed she could use this information to solve her problem. If she was no longer called Paddy, then she would not be subjected to "Paddy, do this." or "Paddy, don't do that."She had the glimmerings of a plan, but it required patience and courage. At church on Sunday, whilst the congregation were "ploughing fields and scattering", she was thinking her plan through and when Monday morning came round, she felt she was ready.

She went to school as normal, but when Miss Fyres took the register, Paddy nervously put her great plan into action.

"Paddy Gibbons?" Paddy didn't acknowledge her name. "Paddy Gibbons!" shouted Miss Fyres once more and again Paddy was silent; she found something very interesting on her desktop and fixed her eyes firmly to it. There was a hush in the classroom. Miss Fyres loomed over her. "Paddy Gibbons!" The shout this time was accompanied by a hard slap round the head. Paddy again stayed dumb and quite still. The class was getting very excited now; Miss Fyres had never been so totally ignored before. She ordered Paddy to go to the Headmaster.

The Headmaster was renowned for the discipline in his school, which was paternal, without being patronising. He was also well known for his mode of transport, Mr Norman lived in a village about three miles out of town and rode to school every day on a bicycle, not very unusual in the days when buses were few and far between, but this bike had a saddle that wasn't fixed, and would swing from side to side with the rhythm of the pedals. It was the first time she had really seen the Headmaster up close, and although she was trembling, she did notice his very large bushy eyebrows hid kindly, far seeing eyes. He was scarcely bigger than her, but commanded respect from everyone.

"Now Paddy, what's this I hear?" She remained silent and looked very firmly at her shoes as if seeing them for the first time. He tried again, "Paddy, what's wrong?" Paddy really wanted to tell him, but she knew she must get this right. Mr Norman was getting concerned now as this was way outside his point of reference; he had never encountered a girl, one who was usually reticent and malleable if her teachers were to be believed, who could be so defiant, and he was intrigued. "Now girl, what is this?" he asked, coming to stand stood next to her.

Paddy heard the magic word "girl", and so was quite ready to tell him that she was now to be called Marlene. Mr Norman was taken aback. He stared at her for a while, wondering what to do. "What do you mean?" he asked. Paddy gazed at him for a while and then, with fear and trembling and a great deal of hesitation, told him that she had decided that, because everyone told her off, saying "Paddy do this or Paddy don't do that", she was no longer to be called Paddy. There was silence. Paddy hadn't got this far in her plan and so had no idea what to do or say next. Mr Norman had no idea either so in desperation he telephoned the Home. Paddy heard Mr Norman say, "yes," and "no" and "I suppose not" and then he put the phone down and stared at her for a long time. He eventually said, that Sister Maude had admitted that it was no use trying to do anything as once Paddy had made up her mind to do something, there was nothing anyone could do, and he suggested they'd better give the news to Miss Fyres. Paddy didn't want to tell Miss Fyres, but followed Mr. Norman, in the hope that he would deal with it.

They went together back into the classroom and both Mr Norman and Miss Fyres left the classroom. When Miss Fyres returned, Paddy gazed at her feet, not daring to look at her. Miss Fyres said with as much factiousness as she could muster, "Marlene, go back to your seat. Yes class, Paddy has now decided to be Marlene!! Is there anyone else who wishes to change their name or anything else for that matter?"

Paddy said nothing, but inside she was puzzled when she should have been triumphant. Was this it? This was her new beginning, what she'd planned for so meticulously, so why didn't she feel really happy? It was what she wanted, so why did it not feel good? She had achieved the success she thought she wanted, triumphed in a most spectacular way so why was she so melancholy? Paddy had all unknowingly learnt that we might think we want something, but it doesn't necessarily mean that we should have it or that if we accomplish it, it will make us happy. So Marlene it was for the next thirty-five years!

Marlene was walking home at lunchtime; this was one of the few times they didn't have to be in a crocodile so Marlene should have been enjoying the walk, but she wasn't. She couldn't remember exactly when she had started to dread lunchtimes, forever she thought, or at least as far back as she could remember. Marlene hoped it would be macaroni cheese as although she didn't like it, she could manage to eat it before the rest of the girls had cleared away. Somehow she just couldn't eat meat; she'd tried drinking lots of water to try to swallow the meat, but that seldom worked as she just got full up with water! She could eat the potatoes, even if they did look like dirty snow, or slush, and she could usually manage the vegetables. She couldn't understand why eating meat was so difficult and wondered if it was because of the night noises, but surely they were fixed and tied to the night when everyone was asleep? She arrived home and went slowly into the refectory. Marlene's heart sank. It was meat!

Twenty minutes later, she was sitting in the chapel hall, her tears making puddles on the plate, still trying to eat her dinner. Sister Maud said she was a wicked, ungrateful girl and Marlene supposed she must be as her dinner was still on the plate. She was told to take her dinner to the Library where the staff were having their lunch, and, as she was trying to eat her dinner, looked out on to the Sisters' garden and wished with all her heart she was out there, instead of looking at her plate and seeing that the dinner was not getting any smaller. Eventually Marlene was told to run back to school, but by the time she got there she was late and so she was in trouble there too. At teatime her uneaten dinner was put in front of her and the sorry charade was acted out again. At breakfast time, Marlene was handed her dinner yet again, and this time managed to swallow nearly all of the remaining meat. She was too late to have a proper breakfast as the girls had started to go into chapel for their morning service. This seemed to be the pattern of almost every meal. Now and again Sister Maude would change all their places in the refectory and Marlene would pray she would sit near someone like Dilly or Moira, both of whom were always hungry and would eat her dinner as well as their own however the swap from her full plate to their empty plate had to be made carefully, so that none of the staff and Sisters knew, and this was sometimes well nigh impossible, as some of the girls would not hesitate to report her and then both parties would get in to trouble. Thus every day the whole sorry mess was re-enacted, month after month, year after year.

The Home 1946

1st row: far right Paddy, Bille next to her then Ethel.

2nd row: far right Mary Jackman, Joyce 3rd right.

Paddy aged 7 1948

Chapter 10: Several Invitations and a Stranger

Marlene's birthday had come and gone, and so had Lent; all the girls were encouraged to "give up" something for Lent, which didn't present much difficulty as you either gave up marmite or marmalade for breakfast or jam for tea. Marlene had decided to give up jam at teatime, as very often she would still be eating her dinner at teatime or even breakfast time; most days the problem of why she couldn't eat her dinner overshadowed everything else and it was only when she was at school she could forget it. It was now Good Friday. They'd been at church all morning and the Sisters stayed at church and fasted until three o'clock. The girls had their traditional Good Friday lunch of Fish Pie and Rice Pudding always eaten off the same plate so as to save time and work. Marlene always enjoyed the lunch as she was able to eat it; fish could be swallowed more easily than meat so she avoided her usual problems. Easter Sunday dawned and staff, Sisters and girls ate breakfast and lunch together. Breakfast was the same as any other feast day, ham, rolls and marmalade: it was like Christmas, without the magic!

There was a new member of staff, in fact a most extraordinary person. Sister Maude introduced her to the girls at teatime. She was dwarfish, almost the same size as Bille, but there was something about her which troubled Marlene: the woman didn't seem to smile with her eyes, although the rest of her face seemed pleasant enough. She was adult, quite stocky, with nondescript hair and a round face and seemed to be sizing up the girls, looking particularly at the older, bigger girls. Sister Maud introduced her as Miss Guy, and she scowled as she heard her name perhaps as a warning to some of the girls not to make fun of her name or her stature. For some reason she looked in particular at Bille! Apparently Miss Guy knew Sister Helena-Mary, but she didn't seem to talk with the same soft burr Sister Helena-Mary did so she couldn't really be Scottish. Marlene used to go to the Nursery every evening to tell stories she had made up to the "littlies", but when Miss Guy was on duty, she didn't feel comfortable doing it. Miss Guy had an invalid vehicle and she would take some of the girls out past the golf course, almost to the next village. There was just room to crouch down between Miss Guy's legs and the cover would hide you from the public eye, but although Marlene went once, again she didn't feel happy about it, so didn't go again.

After the Easter holidays, the school introduced a summer activity, country dancing. Marlene loved it and she made a new friend, though whether you could have a teacher as a friend she wasn't sure. Mrs Richards only took them for country dancing and Marlene had not met her before. She seemed to be younger than Miss Fyres and always seemed to be smiling. She had blond hair and instead of the tight bun which most of the women teachers had, she had curls down to her shoulders and merry blue eyes. Marlene was lucky to be put near Mrs Richards in quite a lot of the dances and she loved both the dances and Mrs Richards. The music, combined with the dance steps, swept her away; she had never danced before, had never seen anyone dancing and Marlene revelled in it.

One Saturday after lunch, instead of going for another dreary walk in the crocodile, Marlene was told by Sister Maude to put on her best clothes as she was going out for tea. Marlene couldn't believe it; no one had ever been invited to tea before, but even though she was excited, she was still apprehensive. She realised it would be more than two slices of bread and jam, but had no idea what anybody else did at teatime. Marlene, in common with all the girls, was not very sure about being able to do anything outside the routine they followed year in and year out. When they were just doing what they'd always done, no one had to think about it, they were "safe". But actually going out to tea! Suppose they had meat? Marlene couldn't have it cold for breakfast as she wouldn't be there at breakfast. She hadn't been told who had invited her and why.

Marlene was ready and waiting in the Sisters hall at two thirty, well, a little after two thirty because she had been beset by worries. Sister Maude was talking to someone who sounded familiar and when the door opened, Marlene wore the biggest smile ever. It was

Mrs Richards. Mrs Richards smiled at her and gave her a hug in spite of Sister Maude's disapproving frown. It was the first hug she could ever remember having, apart from Doreen's hugs, so Marlene hugged her back and then they were on their way. They had a car because Mrs Richards' husband was a doctor; Marlene had never been inside a car before. She looked at the gleaming chrome work and the leather seats and was sure the Queen never had such a luxurious mode of transport. They drove up past the golf club where the girls walked every Sunday and came to a small house; at least Marlene thought it was small when she compared it to the Home. When Mr Richards opened the door, a big fluffy ginger cat greeted them. Marlene asked if she could stroke it and Mrs Richards laughed and said of course she could. Tea was on the table and what a tea! There was jelly and tiny sandwiches and real cake, not Christmas cake. She was pleased Mrs Richards asked her if she liked jelly, but as she wasn't sure whether she'd had jelly before, she just gave a nod. She kept a weather eye on Mrs and Mr Richard, so she would know when and how to eat it and she found it absolutely delicious. Mr and Mrs Richards asked Marlene about her sisters and her life in the Home and after tea they took her into the garden. Marlene just gazed and gazed. She had never had a tea like that and she had never seen such a beautiful garden. It wasn't only seeing the flowers, even though they were beautiful: some of them were scented, and the colours, the perfume and the lazy buzzing of the bees meant she had no words, nor could she move closer as she seemed to be rooted to the spot. Marlene was at peace, but more than that: it was as though she was part of this wonderful world, part of nature itself. She had come home!

On the way home, they were all very quiet. Marlene because she was still lost in the beauty of the whole afternoon, but Mr and Mrs Richards seemed anxious and apprehensive. If Marlene had been herself, she would have been aware of the tense atmosphere. When they arrived home, after Sister Maude had told her to "run along", Mrs Richards kissed and hugged her and Mr Richards hugged her too and both of them went into Sister Maude's office. Marlene ran to look for Doreen to tell her about her wonderful afternoon, but though she ran all over the house searching, she couldn't find her. She saw

Miss Howkins and asked if she knew where Doreen was. It was then Miss Howkins told her Doreen had gone! Marlene didn't understand; why had Doreen not told her and said good-bye? Doreen was her friend. She couldn't just leave and not say good-bye. She ran to find Sister Helena Mary as she was quite sure Miss Howkins was mistaken, Doreen wouldn't go back to Scotland without telling her, but when she found Sister Helena Mary, she told Marlene the same story. Doreen had indeed gone back to Scotland and had caught the train that very afternoon. Marlene was bereft and inconsolable. How could she not tell Doreen about her beautiful afternoon? Doreen had taught her that a joy shared becomes even more joyous and that joy can be repeated again and again with the words, "Do you remember?" but without that sharing, it was very difficult, or even well nigh impossible to hold on to the experience.

Marlene cried all that night and the magical afternoon with Mrs Richards seemed just a memory, a dream. When she returned to school, Mrs Richards had also gone, and later it was left to Dawn to tell her that Mrs Richards had wanted to adopt her. Marlene didn't understand what "adopt" meant, but Dawn also explained it meant to live with Mr and Mrs Richards and be their little girl, for ever and ever. She asked Dawn whether she'd mind if she went away to be Mrs Richards little girl, but Dawn said that as long as she had three big dolls that they could play with as much as they liked, and as long as she and Bille were invited for tea, that was fine. A few days later, Dawn came to find her and said that Sister Maude had refused to allow it as she had said that the three sisters must be together. Marlene had glimpsed the life she might have had and realised that life in the Home was very different. She became very withdrawn, visiting the chapel to such a degree, that apart from her work, and sleeping and eating, she spent all her time in the chapel, reading or just sitting and thinking. It was a bad time for Marlene.

Her birthday had come and gone, and apart from the jobs she had to do and the terrible meal times, Marlene was mostly on her own. One morning Sister Maude came to see her, Dawn and Bille. She explained that some girls in an orphanage in another country wanted to be "pen pals". Marlene asked Dawn what pen pals were and Dawn muttered something about friendship, but it was obvious Dawn didn't really know. If Marlene hadn't been so keen to find out what pen pals were, she could have had a field day, as it was very rare that Dawn didn't know something.

She went to find Miss Howkins, who explained that pen pals were friends who you got to know all about by writing to them. Marlene tapped on the "office" door and told Sister Maude she wanted to have a pen pal, so Sister Maude duly gave her some writing paper, a pen and ink. She wasn't sure what to write so asked Dawn, who was also writing to her "friend". Dawn said she was writing about horses and Marlene thought that this time Dawn had really lost it: what on earth did Dawn know or care about horses? She wondered if she should write about books, but then thought if her "friend" was in another country, she may not have been able to read any English books. Then she wondered if she should write about flowers, but may be her friend didn't like flowers. It had taken a while before Marlene had accepted that some people not only didn't particularly like flowers, but also actually didn't "see" them.

Marlene remembered something a missionary told them when she visited the Home to talk about her work in Africa. She explained that when Africans met anybody, they would shout out, "I see you", meaning not only did they "see" the person by looking at her, but also really "saw" her, recognising her as a person and seeing her as a potential friend. Marlene had thought this wonderful, but wasn't sure she could say this to everyone: could she really recognise Moira as a friend? It would take some doing and she would have to be ready to take flight or use her "look"! She had devised her "look" as she realised that she could be bullied because she was usually on her own. Marlene knew she wasn't good at fighting, so she had thought up this ploy and, to her surprise, it worked. If someone, often Moira, started, she would just stare at her, putting all the hatred she could muster into the "look". The bully was so surprised at this reaction that she usually backed off. In fact, some believed she was capable, not exactly of witchcraft, but of something similar and certainly the "look" worried and upset those girls who meant her harm. This belief was reinforced because after she tried out her chosen weapon on Moira, Moira fell down some stairs. She wasn't really hurt, but as it happened directly after the "look", many girls thought it wasn't accidental, which helped Marlene immensely.

However, she still had to write this letter. Marlene thought about what her pen pal would like to know about her and decided it would probably be how she and her sisters came to the Home and why. That didn't work as she hadn't the faintest idea when or why they'd come to the Home, so what else could she write about? Perhaps she could tell her pen pal how many sisters she had, what sort of things they learnt at school, and what she liked to do. Having finished the letter, Marlene took it to Sister Maude and asked her what country this pen pal came from. Sister Maude hesitated, then, watching her face carefully, told her it was Germany, in a town called Dresden. Sister Maude continued to watch Marlene's face closely when she said this and, when there was no reaction, told her that Dresden had been badly bombed in the war. Still getting no reaction from Marlene, she said she would send the letter off the next day.

A week or so later, Sister Maude gave her an envelope. In fact, it was almost a small package. On opening it, Marlene discovered a small carved white flower on a black velvet ribbon. She asked Sister Maude about the flower, as she had never seen a flower like this one, and Sister Maude told her it was Edelweiss. Marlene put it on quickly and ran to find Miss Howkins to show her it. There was also a letter written in a foreign language, which Sister Eleanor would be able to translate. Sister Eleanor told her that her pen pal's name was Olga and she went to school in Dresden, though at the time of writing this letter, they had to meet in the teacher's house as their school had been bombed! Olga's letter went on to thank her for her letter, and informed her she had two brothers, one who lived with her in a Home and another brother, Ernst, who was missing. She wore her necklace all that day, but when she looked for it in the morning it had gone, where she didn't know, but as all her gifts were ever only with her for a day, she didn't worry about the loss. Marlene wrote another letter thanking Olga and asking questions about the Home she lived in and her school. She waited for a reply, but was disappointed and, as neither Dawn nor Bille had written to their pen pals, that was that.

Chapter 11: The Great Escape

Time went by although Marlene wasn't really aware of it as the days passed quickly in the monotony of routine. School was over for another year and most of the girls were spending the long summer holiday with their parents. After lunch one sunny day, Sister Maude came into the refectory and said she wanted to speak to everybody, though there weren't that many bodies to talk to. Sister Maude looked almost happy and told them that for the very first time, they were all going on holiday, every one! Marlene was apprehensive; after all, she hadn't got a bucket and spade and would she like ice cream? Sister Maude went on to tell them that they were going on holiday to Knebworth, where they were to stay in a big Rectory. Apparently the priest who lived in the Rectory had invited them all to stay while he and his family were on holiday. Marlene went up to Sister Maude and asked about the buckets and spades and ice cream, but Sister Maude almost laughed and said it wasn't that kind of holiday.

The charabanc was to come the next morning and Miss Darnell, the seamstress, wanted to see everyone in turn so she could sort out the clothes they needed to take. The day passed in a whirl, but Marlene did manage to see Tom and tell him about the proposed holiday; he said he knew and he was going to have a holiday as well. He was, "gonna take me Bessie on the chara." Marlene was intrigued, as she'd never heard of a "chara" before, and asked Tom to explain, but all he said was, he'd "gorra ge' on," as he had to clean "me tools, afor I be goin." She went to find Dawn, as she usually knew everything, but Dawn didn't know what a "chara" was either, although she didn't exactly say that, but said, "Don't you even know that?" which Marlene knew translated as "I really don't know, but I'm not going to admit it!"

The next day dawned, promising to be hot, and at breakfast the girls were told to congregate in the chapel hall at eleven o' clock so they would have plenty of time to do their jobs. Sister Maude also threatened that anyone not doing her job would be left behind so everywhere was sparkling and clean by the time they had to be on their way. Marlene wondered how Sister Maude could leave anyone on her own in the house. The big ones had to count the parcels of clothes to make sure everyone had one. They all met in the chapel hall at 10:50. Long minutes ticked by as they waited for Sister Maude to come and tell them everything was ready. At last she came and put all the girls in a special crocodile, the "front" door was opened and they had their first look at the "chara". It seemed very big to Marlene, but as she'd never seen one before, she assumed it was the right size for a charabanc! The girls filed out and went up the steps and into the "chara", after Sister Maude had outlined the sort of behaviour that was expected on the journey. Marlene was sitting next to Bille, who kept wriggling about and demanding to sit next to the window, but Marlene would not give up her seat, saying that Sister Maude had told her to sit there. Bille looked thunderous, but was soon having a chat with Donna and the window seat was forgotten.

The journey didn't take as long as Marlene wanted, as she was thoroughly enjoying looking out of the window and seeing all sorts of activities which, when walking in a crocodile, she always missed. She saw some men in a field harvesting the corn and some rabbits running across the same fields; she saw some children looking for blackberries and wanted to tell them it was too early and she saw other children in a park laughing and running and free.

The "chara" suddenly stopped and Sister Maude stood up and told them that they had to unlock the gates before the bus could get in. Some of the big girls ran forward, but Sister Maude told everyone to sit down, as Betty would have that honour. Eventually they got to the house, and Sister Maude told everyone to get out of the bus and line up outside the house, It was a big house, but not as big as the Home, and Marlene kept dodging about so she could get a better look. Unfortunately everyone else had the same idea and she expected Sister Maude to put them in a crocodile so they could enter the house decorously, but Sister Maude almost smiled again and after Miss Howkins had opened the door, they all piled in.

There was an entrance hall, which wasn't as big as the one at the Home, and Sister Maude directed them to the room she called the "Morning Room". There were lists on a notice board that showed the rota for laying the table, clearing the table and washing up for breakfast, dinner and tea. There was also a plan of the upper floors: like the Home the house had three storeys, but didn't have a "Tube". Marlene was pleased about that because the Tube was cold and eerie and she never felt safe there. She looked at the plan and saw it also had names near all the rooms and Dawn said it was where they were going to sleep. Marlene looked in vain for her name; she asked Dawn to find it, but she couldn't see it either. Very soon all the girls were pushing and shoving to try and find Marlene's name and all of a sudden Dora called out that she knew where it was. She pointed to a room and Marlene's heart sank. There was silence from everyone. Marlene's name was underneath Sister Maude's. She was very apprehensive, but Bille immediately saw new and exciting possibilities in this extraordinary situation. For as long as she could remember, all the girls had been curious to know what the nuns looked like without their veils, and now Bille reasoned they couldn't possibly go to bed in their veils, so it was the ideal time to discover what nuns did have under the veils.

Marlene had other worries: supposing the night noises came or the snakes? Even worse was the thought that her bed might be wet and cold when she woke up. Bille didn't even consider this and offered to swap places with her, as first hand knowledge would be much better. Bille knew what a wonderful story this would make and she also knew that she wouldn't tell everybody straight away. She thought of all the ways she could profit from this knowledge, especially as the girls who had been on holiday with their families often came home with chocolates and sweets which they were usually unwilling to share. Bille asked Sister Maude, but Sister Maude looked at Bille's black eyes sparkling with wickedness and refused to make the change. Marlene was dreading bedtime, but as usual it came too soon. Bille had had to go to bed earlier, but had grabbed her and fiercely whispered that Marlene wasn't to tell anyone else what was underneath Sister Maud's veil.

Marlene went slowly into the bedroom after having had a wash in, what seemed to her, a rather small bathroom. All the girls were keeping to the very specific rota Sister Maude had made so that they all were washed and ready for bed in the right order and there were no big queues for bathroom or toilets. Sister Maude was canny enough to know from experience that "the devil makes work for idle hands". Marlene looked around and saw the room was very tiny in comparison to the dormitory at the Home and had two beds; she wasn't sure which bed was hers, but, as she was dithering, she noticed a Bible on one of the beds, so she assumed that was Sister Maude's. Marlene hastily got into bed and shut her eyes so she wouldn't see Sister Maude as she really couldn't imagine what you could say to a nun without a veil, not that she knew what to say to one when she had a veil! After some time, she heard the door open, and peeked out of one eye, but she saw Sister Maude watching her so shut her eyes tightly, and the next time she opened them, bright light streamed in at the window and Sister Maude's bed was empty. Where had the night noises gone? There had been no sign of the snakes, and her bed was dry and warm. Bille accosted her as soon as she saw her and demanded answers, but Marlene had to confess she had slept the whole night and hadn't woken up till morning. Poor Bille, seeing all the chocolates and sweets slipping away was furious, at least, as furious as you can be when you're six and look four, but she gave Marlene one more chance.

After breakfast she went up to her room to tidy the bed and drifted over to the window to look at the garden; it was full of bright flowers, but was not as beautiful as Mrs.Richard's. She wouldn't think about that she told herself fiercely, wiping a tear away. Marlene noticed that beyond the garden was a wooded area, and she hoped they would be allowed to go into the wood; she'd never been in a wood, indeed she'd never seen a real one. The bell rang and they all congregated in the "morning room" as they'd been told to do. Miss

Howkins told them they could explore the garden, but not the wood. All the girls dived for the door, pushing each other in their haste, but Bille was first as always. She was easily the smallest, but could use her feet and hands to kick and punch in a very determined fashion; indeed many rugby players could have taken lessons from her!! Bille made straight for a yew tree that had been damaged in a storm, as one of the branches was lying horizontal to the ground. She was soon up on that branch and then the next and was now swinging like a monkey from a branch that was as tall as Reverend Mother. Bille had no fear at all. Donna immediately ran and got Miss Howkins and while everyone was fussing around and Miss Howkins was once again rescuing Bille, Marlene slipped into the wood.

It was dark after the bright sunny garden, and as she ventured further into the wood, the sounds of the girls' laughter were gradually left behind. Soon everywhere was silent except for the wind soughing through the trees and the birds singing. Marlene stopped and was part of the wood and nature itself; she hardly dare take a breath in case the spell was broken. She sat down and heard the rustling of small animals and wondered what they were, but decided it didn't really matter, as they too were part of this alternative universe. After a while Marlene got up and starting wandering deeper in to the wood; she didn't really think of the direction she was going in and gradually the wood became cold and the light that had been streaming through the trees was gone. Suddenly, Marlene realised she was lost and the feeling of being a part of this natural world was also lost. The wood felt alien, almost ghostly as there was so little light coming through the trees and she was frightened. She tried to find the way she had come from, but only succeeded in becoming convinced she would never find the way out. Marlene felt cold inside and ran this way and that, but to no avail. She panicked and was crying and desperate as she realised that no one knew she was in the wood. Suddenly she heard a voice in the distance calling her name. Marlene shouted as loudly as she could, but the voices became fainter and fainter until she couldn't hear them any longer. She was bereft. She had no idea what she could do and then suddenly, she knew she wasn't alone; there was no need to panic. The presence Marlene felt would not let any real danger come to her. She had no idea who or what the presence was, but it didn't matter, for as long as she trusted this inner self, this presence, she would be all right. She stood quite quietly waiting, perfectly calm and, now she was no longer frightened, the wood seemed at one with her once more.

Marlene suddenly knew what path to take, so without wondering whether it seemed right, she took it. Gradually the wood grew lighter, and now she could clearly hear the girls calling her. Sister Maud was cross, but not as cross as Marlene thought she'd be, and although she was sent to bed without any tea. Marlene didn't mind as she was in the middle of "Uncle Tom's cabin" and had started thinking about the life of the slaves.. The door opened just as Marlene settled down; Bille had brought her some bread and jam. Marlene was amazed Bille could be so thoughtful and brave, as if she was found out there would be trouble for Bille as well, but when she reminded Marlene of the necessity of getting the information she wanted, Marlene knew Bille hadn't turned over a new leaf and wasn't ill: she was just being her normal self.

When they got home, the other girls started drifting back from their holidays. Bille who had not managed to get the information about Sister Maude, made it all up and managed to bribe several girls to give her some goodies before she told them the "greatest story" ever, and so the summer ended. When they returned to school, much to hers and everyone's surprise, Marlene managed to shout out about her holiday before Brian Merril got the chance. Marlene also found, much to her amazement, that she was going to room with Dilly. This was very unusual, as normally the girls stayed in the dormitory until they were at least ten. Another surprise was that the night noises appeared to be gone, and she wasn't quite such a "dirty, smelly, Home kid" as she'd thought.

Chapter 12: Murder, Escape, Gifts and a Stranger

Marlene was in the schoolroom, where all the girls were promoted to at the age of eight, leaving the nursery behind. After her birthday she had spent more time with the other girls, though she still escaped to the chapel or the apple tree in the back garden, either to read or just "be". The reason she was spending more time in the schoolroom was that Sister Helena Mary had taught her to knit. Sister Helena Mary was a great knitter, even knitting when she had to supervise the girls at mealtimes and she could keep up with what was going on and knit at the same time. Sister Eleanor was standing in the doorway trying to attract the girls' attention. This took some time, for Sister Eleanor did not command the same respect as Sister Maude, Sister Helena Mary or Miss Howkins; indeed most girls totally ignored Sister Eleanor.

Marlene wondered why some people could walk into a room and there was instant silence, whereas other people, like Sister Eleanor, could shout and shout and people still wouldn't listen. Not that Sister Eleanor would ever shout. It had nothing to do with a loud voice, as Sister Helena Mary had an even quieter voice than Sister Eleanor, and it had nothing to do with size - Sister Helena-Mary was very tiny. But there was something, some sign which was invisible and inaudible, but was there, and everybody recognised it. Eventually the girls were quieted, though whether this was because of Sister Eleanor, or Sister Maud's scowling face as she passed by the schoolroom, it was difficult to tell.

Sister Maud's large and very ancient dog needed a walk and so she had sent Sister Eleanor to ask for a volunteer amongst all the girls over the age of 10. After she asked the girls, the silence stretched and stretched and, as no one offered, Marlene, who felt sorry for Sister Eleanor, almost volunteered. She was reading "Rebecca" and she was about to find out whether she was going to do about the evil Mrs. Danvers. She waited for a while, but nothing happened, so she reluctantly put up her hand. Sister Eleanor looked at her uncertainly. Sister Maude had been very specific about the age of the "dog walker", and

Marlene was only eight, but she was sensible and no one else had volunteered, so Sister Eleanor decided, fatefully, to take a chance. Sister Eleanor went over the proposed route carefully, "up the Crescent, down Tavistock Road, then up Union Street and then turning into Bromham Road. She didn't have to cross any roads and the whole walk should take no more than 10 minutes. Marlene fetched both the lead and Bob and set out. She was very proud and smiled at every one she met so they could see how grown-up she was to be allowed to take a dog for a walk! One or two people stopped and talked to her, stroking Bob as they talked. When she and Bob were on their own, she chattered happily to him. She'd passed the Crescent and had nearly arrived at Union Street when disaster struck! Bob slipped his lead and ran into the road in the path of an oncoming car. Bob squealed and whimpered and then went very still. Marlene lost all sense of reason; she knelt beside Bob crying and imploring him to wake up. She was quite safe from traffic as few people had cars. Eventually she realised he was dead; shaking all over, and still holding the lead, Marlene knew she couldn't go home. She had been punished often in her short life for many things, but what would happen if Sister Maude found out she'd murdered Bob, Sister Maud's own dog, who had lived at the Home longer than even she had? Suddenly she knew what she had to do. She had to run away, but where to? She was in Clapham Road, so although she had never been to Clapham, this road must lead there, so sniffling and shaking, she started on the journey. Marlene gave no thought to what she would do when she arrived at Clapham. She just ran and ran.

A car stopped beside her, but Marlene gave no thought to it, scarcely seeing it in her distress. The driver wound down the window, speaking to her, but she didn't, couldn't and wouldn't hear him. He idled the car to keep up with her and spoke louder, but again she was deaf and blind in her panic. The car stopped and the man got out, running with her and talking, then shouting at her, but again Marlene couldn't, wouldn't, see him. Eventually he caught hold of her arm, but she shook it off and crying even louder and running even faster, she evaded him. After some time he managed to catch Marlene and she remained still. The driver told her he was the owner of the car that had hit Bob and asked her where she was going. She told him she couldn't go home as she'd done such a terrible thing! He asked her where she lived and she told him, so he offered to take her home. Marlene cried louder and tried to free herself so she could run again. He held her more tightly; he sensed her fear had to be caused by more than the death of the dog, as most children, after such a terrible experience, would immediately want to go home. He questioned Marlene gently, allowing her to take her time, and when she was calmer, she explained that her punishment would be terrible. When she saw he didn't believe her, she told him about the whippings and other punishments for quite mild misdemeanours. He told her he was a doctor and that she must go home and he would explain to Sister Maude, and she would not be punished.

When they arrived back at the Home, he related the whole sad story to Sister Maude. Sister Maude told Marlene to go to the schoolroom, but, tired out physically and mentally, she sought solace in the chapel. By some miracle, most of the whippings stopped after this. Marlene still had to struggle through dinner times and it was a rare day that she didn't have to eat her dinner at teatime, but though she rarely managed to eat it at tea-time she seldom had to eat her dinner cold at breakfast, but her plate was always washed by her tears. Dawn told her later, much later when they had both left the Home to seek their fortune in the great wide world, that Sister Maude had told all the girls that they must never mention the incident and as a measure of the respect the girls had for Sister Maude, they never did.

Paddy had noticed that Sister Helena Mary's knitting was very different from her usual style. The colours were more vibrant and instead of the usual straight lines, this knitting was an unusual shape and it didn't seem to be as big as it generally was. Also Sister Helena Mary had to keep referring to some paper with lots of words on it that Marlene couldn't decipher. One glorious day Marlene caught a falling leaf and knew she could wish for anything she wanted. She had been late, so was some way behind the "crocodile" and then she had seen the leaf. It almost flew in to her outstretched hand and she had grasped it firmly. She finally had her "good luck charm" and she could have anything she wanted, but as she knew the chances of getting another charm were practically nil, she had to use it carefully. Marlene thought about having some chocolate, but she'd seen how Dilly suddenly got lots and lots of "friends" and sometimes also threats when she had chocolates. Marlene deliberated about having a garden, but then dismissed it, as she knew the others would either spoil it on purpose or would run on it by accident. Marlene could think of nothing she would really like to have as a result of her "good luck"! Poor Marlene had learnt the sad truth that when your dreams come true, they seldom bring the pleasure you had envisaged. In the end, she decided to use the leaf as a bookmark, as it was very pretty!

Winter was upon them heralded by Dawn's bleeding hands. Sister Eleanor said she had chilblains, but that was no help to Dawn. She seldom cried about them, but this year they were even worse! One Saturday, after a very heavy snowstorm, the girls decided they would go to their garden to play snowballs. They had done their jobs, and were very surprised when a window opened and Sister Helena Mary told them they could all go into the front garden as the snow was thicker there, all of them that is except Marlene, Bille and Dawn, who were told to come inside. All three of them were concerned; Marlene and Dawn were mystified, as they couldn't think of anything they had done wrong. Bille, as usual, looked guilty, but vehemently protested her innocence, even though she didn't know what she was being accused of, but because she was Bille there would be plenty of misdemeanours to choose from! Sister Helena Mary was waiting in the schoolroom and had an embroidered bag with her. When they were all settled, she drew from the bag the mysterious knitting she'd been doing for weeks and gave them all Tam O'Shanters and gloves. They looked at the strange berets and Helena Mary said that they were always worn like that in Scotland. The three sisters were thrilled with their presents, and after Sister Helena Mary had helped them put them on, they too were allowed to go into the hallowed front garden.

The snowballing had finished and most of the girls had gone in, but Moira was still outside rolling a huge ball of snow. The three sisters were soon rolling their own balls which became very big indeed. Suddenly their names were called and turning to face Sister Eleanor they realised that photos were being taken. This was such a rare occasion that Bille, in particular, played and posed for the camera.

It turned out to be the coldest winter on record; poor Dawn's hands were evidence of this as, covered in chilblains, each and every morning when she went to school, they were dripping with blood! Christmas came and went, but because of the heavy snowfalls the snowdrops were hidden for so long that when the snow finally melted, the snowdrops were over for another year. It was her birthday in two weeks but Marlene wasn't really looking forward to it. It was nice to receive presents on the day, but by the next day they had vanished. Then, on a Saturday afternoon, a message came from Sister Maude that the three sisters were to go to Miss Howkins to be tidied and then report to Sister Maude in the library. This was very strange, for although the girls with mothers were often summoned in this way, the three sisters had never had any visitors. All three of them were nonplussed, but Miss Howkins was waiting so they went straight away.

Marlene and Dawn were soon ready, hair tidy, clothes neat, but Bille wasn't. She had changed and looked like she was ready for Miss Howkins to do her hair, but Bille was never ready where her hair was concerned. It was fine, silky, short, blue/black hair, and was the cause of a daily battle between Bille and Miss Howkins. They both took up their positions and battle commenced. Years ago, Miss Howkins had resorted to a brush, as combs took longer, so armed with Bille's brush, (she was the only girl in the Home to have a brush), Miss Howkins took a firm hold on Bille, and it began. Miss Howkins actually managed to get the brush to Bille's hair - one up to Miss Howkins. However seconds later Bille was trying to run from the room, but Miss Howkins had too tight a hold on her. Sister Maude had told Miss Howkins to get as far away from the Library as possible and this proved wise, as Bille, thwarted by Miss Howkins' tight hold, started wailing and screaming like a banshee. Most people would have been so horrified by the dreadful screams that they would have loosened their hold, but not Miss Howkins. This was phase two of the battle, and then came the end game: Bille was shaking her head to prevent her hair being brushed, as well as screeching and sobbing, but Miss Howkins clamped her hand on Bille's head and at last the job was done, in record time too! Bille regained her chirpy personality in seconds and with a quick wipe of Bille's face, Miss Howkins was victorious. They were ready!

They arrived at the library door and there was then the usual battle as to who had the bad luck to go first; it was really only between Dawn and Marlene as, through long experience, Bille was never allowed to go first. If there was to be a disaster, it was far better to let the disaster creep up on you; with Bille it was instant total chaos, especially if the person concerned was not au fait with Bille! Eventually Dawn went first, as she was the eldest, and they entered the library. So began the strangest experience Marlene had ever had! Dawn broke down screaming and sobbing. Marlene didn't know what to feel. It was very reassuring to her that Dawn, the eldest and usually the most confident and sensible sister, could behave in this bizarre fashion, but she was very concerned for Dawn. Dawn then ran to the stranger standing with Sister Maude crying, "Mummy, Mummy!"

This person couldn't be their mother, for one thing she wasn't dressed like a mother; she didn't have big red lips and she certainly didn't have shoes with stilt-like heels like Dilly's mother and the mothers of most of the other girls as well. Marlene stood apart and watched Dawn start hugging and kissing this person, sobbing as she did so. Sister Maude was also beginning to look quite cross and anxious. Sister Maude anxious? Surely not? Marlene looked at Bille, who had also hung back, but when the magic word "Mummy" was heard, Bille immediately "knew" that mummies brought chocolates and Dilly's mum brought lovely "Home-made" chocolates. When they weren't immediately produced, Bille started yelling too, but when you looked closely, there were no tears at all, though it sounded good. The stranger called her, Paddy, but Marlene looked askance. She thought to herself, "She doesn't even know my name," and although she came a little closer, and suffered the hug, she turned away when it became apparent she was to be kissed too. Bille, still looking for the chocolates, put on her most doleful look and her lower lip trembled; she had been practising this, and although people who knew Bille weren't impressed, it was useful at school, or with strangers.

After a short time, Sister Maude sent the girls back to the schoolroom, though Dawn was screaming and crying and holding on to the stranger as if her life depended on it. Marlene was desperately trying to remember everything, as it was turning into an adventure, and one she could regale the other girls with. Marlene had never really had an "adventure", at least not one with a "mother" in it and she had always envied those girls who came back from "proper" holidays with tales of what their mothers had given them and where their mothers had taken them. Strangely enough, there was no mention of fathers, but no one seemed to expect there to be anyway. Now Marlene would have a story to tell! Eventually, Sister Helena Mary came in and managed to pull Dawn and Bille off the stranger and shepherd them out the door. Marlene looked at Dawn incredulously, but Dawn just cried harder! Marlene thought that this was a real "Alice through the Looking Glass" experience: all that was wanted were a dormouse and a mad march hare wearing a hat! Dawn was still insisting that the stranger was indeed their mother, but as she hadn't even known Marlene's name, Marlene was equally convinced she wasn't. Bille, who had been "cheated" out of "her" chocolates sided with Marlene, both of them agreeing that Dawn was completely mad! It was to be another nine years before Marlene discovered that the stranger was indeed their mother.

The Home 1949

Front row: 1st left, Dawn; 3rd left, Marlene; 3rd from right, Donna; far right, Bille.

2nd row: 1st left, Ethel; 3rd left, Miss Guy; 4th from left, Sister Helena-Mary; next to her,

Sister Maud and next to her Miss Howkins; 3rd from right, Maggie; 2nd from right,

Doreen.

3rd row: 1st right, Dora; Pru 3rd row next to Kathleen, Ethel's sister.

4th row: 3rd left, Joyce; far right, Elsie.

Playing with snow January 1950

Bille far right, then Moira, then Dawn with Marlene far left.

Bille at The Home January 1950

Chapter 13: A Friend at Last

It was mid-summer and Sister Helena Mary summoned Marlene. Jobs were done and Marlene had managed, not only to get a pack of cards, but also, by retreating to her usual spot in the corner where the bookshelves ended and the cupboards began, had been able to play some quiet games of patience without being interrupted. Marlene knew she couldn't take the cards out of the schoolroom unless she was going to hand them back to one of the staff, so reluctantly she gave them to Moira. When she arrived at the Sisters' office, Sister Helena Mary smiled at her and introduced her to a "new" girl, Barbara. Marlene was asked to show her round the Home, explaining which areas the girls could use and which they couldn't. This was the sort of job Marlene enjoyed and she gave Barbara a very thorough tour, but hesitated when it came to the Tube, and just waved a hand at the stairs. She took Barbara to meet Miss Darnell, the lady who did the sewing for the Home; she showed Barbara the other end of the Tube and took Barbara to meet Miss Howkins who told Marlene that Barbara would share a dormitory with Bille, as she was Bille's age, and therefore too young to have a proper bedroom. She and Barbara swapped life histories, though Marlene didn't really have one, as all she could remember was being in the Home and thought she may have played "witchy" somewhere else with Bille and Dawn.

Marlene also had a faint memory of a very large meadow; she was there with a man and a woman, but who they were she didn't know. There was a stream as well and she could remember going into the stream and playing until the man fished her out, but whether this really happened or whether it was just a dream she wasn't sure! Marlene also thought she remembered coming to the Home, walking between two adults and being cross, as they kept on talking and walking close to one another for some reason and Marlene was pushed to the front as if she was in a push chair; but that couldn't be right surely? All she really knew was that because Bille was on the inside, she not only had plenty of space, but, more importantly, could hear what the two grown-ups were saying! Marlene instinctively knew she couldn't share these memories with the new girl. They did discover, though, that they both liked books and playing cards; in fact Barbara had a pack of cards with her and from then on they were" bosom" pals".

Marlene had a new teacher, Miss Jones, who although she would never take the place of Mrs Richards, was very kind. She had bright ginger hair and green eyes which seemed to be full of fun, but she still let Brian Merril shout out about Billing Aquadrome, but thankfully "Brer Rabbit" seemed to have been dropped into the well of childhood. However now Marlene had someone to laugh with, it didn't seem so important. She found out that Barbara had a mum who was going to come at Christmas to give her presents. For the whole of that term Marlene was deliriously happy and she and Barbara were inseparable; she didn't go to the chapel by herself anymore and she didn't spend all her time with her head in a book. Barbara's cards had been taken from her, but that didn't seem to matter either. Marlene had a real friend and she could hold her head up high. She wasn't bullied so much either, so all in all, she was happy.

Christmas came and Barbara didn't go to her mother's so Marlene was able to share those delights as well. She thought of Doreen and knew Doreen would be happy for her. She remembered what Doreen had told her about how happiness shared becomes so much greater. Now she had a real friend, she knew this to be true. Marlene was looking forward to her birthday - her tenth - in a week's time. Sister Maude had told Barbara that she was going to spend that Saturday with her mother and she had managed to dash back to tell Marlene. Saturday passed and Sunday and there was no sign of Barbara. Monday morning dawned and Marlene asked Sister Maude where Barbara was. She was then told she had left the Home and wouldn't be coming back! This time Marlene didn't break down, there were no tears, but she was irrevocably changed; she no longer wanted a friend. Marlene knew from now on she would be entirely on her own!

Marlene knew if she were to be on her own, she would have to find some way to deal with the bullying. She had just read a story about a girl who had lived in a very poor part of Glasgow, which was a place in Scotland. She had been bullied, but she had shown no fear and stayed perfectly still while the bullies swung a stone over her head, getting closer to her each time. In the end, the bullies had become bored and stopped. She had become a missionary when she had grown up; Marlene didn't want to do that as she had read countless books with pictures in them depicting exactly what had been done to missionaries. Men who wore only a skirt, or what looked like a skirt, had thrown some of them off cliffs. Marlene had also seen pictures where the missionaries had been tied to poles and trees and the dark men with skirts, had thrown spears at them, so no, she didn't want to do that. She loved the hymn:

> *Over the sea there are little brown children,*
> *Fathers and mothers and babies too.*
> *They haven't heard of the little Lord Jesus.*
> *No on had told them*

Marlene knew it was a missionary hymn, and it did sound very nice being a missionary, but she had seen the pictures and believed them. She really did not want to have spears thrown at her and she certainly didn't want to be thrown from a cliff, which sounded horrible, even though she had never seen a cliff in her whole life.

Marlene knew that ignoring the bullies was not going to be enough; she needed something more, a weapon, but she knew she wasn't any good at fighting, so what was she going to do? "The look", she had devised almost two years ago worked with girls who had been at the Home for some time and for individual girls, but she really needed another weapon particularly for the gangs of three or four girls who sometimes roamed round the Home looking for trouble, and then she suddenly realised the clue was in the story of the girl in Glasgow!

Her chance came a few days later. Ethel, who was usually friendly and therefore not one who had to be avoided, accosted her at the top of the Tube steps. Ethel was with Moira and Rosie. They told her to go down the stairs to allow them to continue on their way. The Tube steps were made of stone and there were some twelve or thirteen steps in all. Marlene stayed where she was, which puzzled them. Then Moira said that they would throw her downstairs unless she backed down and allowed them to pass. Marlene knew that this was the moment to test her theory, so she told them that she was not going down the stairs and they would have to throw her down. Moira took her arm, threatening her, but Marlene just stood firm. After several minutes, the girls, with lots of grumbling and bravado, pretended they were bored with the "game" and let her pass. Marlene had won! She was now even more on her own, but strangely she didn't feel lonely any more. Of course, she wasn't always on her own, as often all the "Home kids" would play a game or do some other activity together, but she no longer had a close friend to share her thoughts with.

Marlene had been reading a book by someone called Lamb who had written a number of short stories. She had just finished one where the uncle had poured poison in his nephew's ear when he was sleeping! She felt extremely frightened and, when she lay down that night, analysed exactly how she slept. Marlene soon realised that her right ear was unprotected and, although common sense told her that she didn't have an uncle and, even if someone came to the Home to do the deed, there were so many bedrooms, as well as two dormitories below her, there was a very slim chance that the mythical uncle would climb the stairs and get to her bedroom. Nevertheless, from that day onward, Marlene always slept with her ears under the bedclothes.

Her birthday came and went. The wallflowers were out and Tom had planted a big border with them at the top of the Sisters' garden. She now used to go and sit in the garden where the wallflowers were. It was difficult to see her from the library as she was behind the shrubbery and, although Tom often walked round the back of the shrubbery, he didn't seem to see her either. One Saturday morning Sister Maude came into the garden. Marlene was sure she would have seen her amongst the wallflowers, but Sister Maude gave no real sign that she had seen her either even though she walked very close to her. Marlene loved the scent of the flowers and often sat amongst them reading or just sitting. She felt a deep peace at this time; she was at one with nature and she knew that this peace would be with her all her life. Marlene also knew that sometimes, even if the conditions were right, she might not be able to feel this deep contentment, that there would be occasions when the "worries of the world" would not let her be, but even though she might not always be able to feel it, this quietude would be hers always.

One of the most beneficial things the girls had was their very capacious navy blue or sometimes white serge knickers. Dawn had found out that the Sisters now had a new larder. It was the other side of the Sisters' hall and had a very thick iron door. Dawn also said that the Sisters were being given the most lovely and delicious food that they kept in the larder. Marlene had very often "borrowed" books from the library as she was by now a voracious reader and she had found that the knickers, indeed, were very versatile and could take three or four books easily; the problem was getting them out of the library without being seen. It was easy in the summer time as, if it was hot, the library French doors would be open and you could enter by the Sisters' garden and escape that way also. As the larder was next door to the library the same escape route could be used. However in winter this route was not possible, so one of the girls would regularly creep up the laundry steps to see what goodies were in the Sister's larder and would inform everybody.

Marlene still shared a bedroom with Dilly on the top floor and one day Betty told everyone she had seen chocolate biscuits in the larder. Marlene offered to get some for a midnight feast. Since the holiday, and since she had moved upstairs out of the dormitory, the night noises had gone, and though she still slept badly, the terrors of the night had abated. Marlene went to the larder by way of the back stairs and put lots of the chocolate biscuits in her knickers making sure some were left so it would be more difficult to see that several were missing; she hurried up to her bedroom and carefully put them in her bed. Although spring had come they were still having very cold frosty nights and so Miss Howkins was still filling the one, and only stone hot water bottle that she would then place in someone's bed. It was entirely random, but you can guess what happened; Miss Howkins placed the hot bottle in Marlene's bed, not knowing of course that the biscuits were there too. When Marlene went to bed and tried to feel the biscuits with her toe, all she encountered was a very warm, sticky mess. She could not believe it; it was rare to find the bottle in her bed as there were 29 other girls who also occasionally would find the bottle in their beds. When Dilly and most of the household were asleep, Marlene had to use the water from the bottle to scrub at the mess which took most of the night before the brown stain of chocolate disappeared. When she had wet her bed at night there was always a punishment, so what would happen if they found the chocolate in her bed? She dared not think. Marlene had to continually take the sheet off the bed and take it on to the landing to see whether the stain had gone and fortunately by the end of the night it was relatively clean, the sheet was back on the bed and all was well. The other girls were very cross and accused her of eating all the biscuits until she told them the real story. Obviously Dilly knew nothing as she'd slept through it all.

Poor Dilly, because of her mental slowness, was the perfect person to play jokes on. Sister Maude once asked her if she would go and fetch something from the butcher's over the road. Dilly was delighted, as if you wanted to send someone reliable, Dilly would not be your first chance, or even your second, but this time she had been chosen! Sister Maude asked Dilly to fetch a tin of "elbow grease" from the butcher. Sister Maude made her practise the message several times until she could remember it and when she had got it word perfect, Sister Maude suddenly had such a bad fit of coughing, Dilly could see tears in Sister Maude's eyes. Dilly was so proud at being sent as a messenger, and repeated the message, word perfect, to the butcher. The butcher asked her to repeat it again, and then he too had a coughing fit. Eventually he gravely asked her to take a message back to Sister Maude. Could Dilly say that he was right out of elbow grease, but could he swap her a silk purse especially made from a pig's ear? Dilly looked round the butcher's shop for the silk purse, but couldn't see one. Long minutes passed until she had it word perfect, and Dilly returned to the Home to give Sister Maude the all-important message! When she repeated the butcher's message, Sister Maude had such a big coughing fit that she just waved Dilly out of her office. Poor Dilly was so worried about the strange noises coming from Sister Maude's office that she told Sister Helena Mary who hurried to see if Sister Maude was all right. Soon the strange noises became louder and Dilly could still hear them as she rejoined the rest of the girls in the schoolroom.

Chapter 14: Ghosties and Ghoulies and Long Legged Beasties

One night most of the girls were woken from their sleep in the early hours of the morning by whistles, men shouting and dogs barking. Suddenly one of the bigger girls, who slept on the top floor, ran down to the younger girls' dormitory on the floor below, and in a stage whisper, told all who were awake to look out of the front window. All of them, except those who "slept like the dead", immediately made a rush to the window. A most peculiar sight met their eyes; even though it was early February and still very dark, the garden was full of light from several torches. There were men running everywhere, and it was twenty minutes or so until the garden was quiet and deserted and the men had gone. Ethel appeared and told everyone she'd heard a prisoner had escaped from the prison down the road, about two hundred yards from the Home, and although she thought the police had recaptured the prisoner, she wasn't really sure. She'd been trying to listen to the staff and nuns below, but the adults were talking so quietly, she couldn't hear properly. At school next day all the Home kids had a red-letter day as, very unusually for them, they had an exciting story to tell, and, as they told the story, each of them embellished it just a little to give them a starring role in the saga. Bille, maybe, went a little over the top as she proudly proclaimed that, yes in her nightie, she had not only captured the man single handed, but also was to get a medal from the police to thank her for all her "daring do". She stared defiantly at anyone who might think it was less than the truth and, as all the action had happened while the bedrooms were still in darkness, no one could say with any certainty, where Bille was!!

The "Boot Room", where the girls kept their wellington boots, was down some steps from the schoolroom. The outside door had a weak latch and so frequently opened by itself, especially if it was very windy. Most of the girls had got into the habit of always checking their wellies before putting them on, as they were an ideal hiding place for cockroaches and spiders. Dilly always forgot and there would be a frightened scream from Dilly as her feet, yet again, encountered one or the other, or sometimes both: it was always good for a laugh. Marlene and Rosie decided to play a trick on poor Dilly. Rosie was Marlene's age, but although they got on, neither was inclined to be the other's "best friend". One morning, when they all putting on their wellies, Dilly gave her usual cry and then turned her boot upside down to reveal a very large cockroach. Rosie immediately turned to Dilly and asked her about her mum, a subject that Dilly could talk for hours. Dilly, delighted at receiving so much attention, and having the chance to "educate" the girls on the wonders of having such a mother, had been practising for months in case she ever got the opportunity. She then regaled the girls with the only subject she knew and settled down to describe the bright red lipstick and the "stilt" heels on her Mum's shoes. She had just got into her stride when someone reminded the girls, and poor Dilly, of the time. The other girls had hung around, as they realised that something was going to happen and happen to poor Dilly.

While Rosie kept Dilly's attention away from her boot, Marlene put the poor cockroach back in to Dilly's Wellington. Again poor Dilly cried out, and once again the trick was played. After the third go Marlene said that she ought to take her boot to Sister Maude as it was obvious that the cockroach had made a nest inside her boot. Dilly, immediately and in floods of tears, went off to tell Sister Maude. When Sister Maude heard the sorry tale, she asked Dilly who she had been talking to and who had been very close to the boot. When she found out it was Marlene and Rosie she sent for them and agreed with them that there was probably a nest of cockroaches inside Dilly's Wellington boot. She then suggested Dilly wear Marlene's boots and sent her off for her walk. When Dilly had gone, Sister Maude turned to Rosie and Marlene and told them that, as it was possible there was indeed a nest of cockroaches, they should clean the boot room from top to bottom, washing the floor and the walls.

They both listened in shocked silence, especially Rosie who was frightened of cockroaches and spiders and so always emptied her boots at arms' length. Marlene wasn't thrilled either as she was reading for the nth time "Froggy's Little Brother" and had just got to the part where the little brother dies. But they had enjoyed the joke and Marlene said she would clean the floor where all the cockroaches generally were, and Rosie could clean the walls. They were both surprised to find that the joke was worth all the cleaning and would probably go down in the annals of the Home as one of the best jokes in the history of the Home.

One November evening Ethel, Moira, Dawn, Rosie and Marlene were sitting in the schoolroom. It was quite dark, both inside and out, as the only light was from the hall outside. Moira had been boasting for some time that her mother had taken her to the cinema in the summer to watch a horror film. As many of the girls "gilded the lily" on returning to the Home after time spent with their parents, this revelation hadn't had the impact Moira felt it should. As a consequence, this particular night, she had decided that they should hear the terrible ghost story come what may. Moira was lucky, as the darkened schoolroom, with the wind blowing loudly outside and the boot room door rattling, was just the setting for her story. In a hushed theatrical tone she began.

Frances was to go to a picnic with her best friend.......

Marlene thought she'd rather be reading "Ivanhoe", a book she'd chosen because of rather a gruesome picture on the first page depicting a fire and people of all ages fleeing with men in armour pursuing them with swords. As this was the only picture in the book, she had no way of knowing whether this was a very minor part of the book, but she had started it and was enjoying it. However she thought she'd give Moira's story a few more minutes.

Moira's voice dropped even more as she told them about Francis and her friend.

Both girls were getting ready to go out. Frances was in the bath and Jacqueline was putting on her make-up in the kitchen. Suddenly a man burst into the bathroom, brandishing a very large knife.....

All the girls, even Marlene, were now listening to the story intently. If anything, the wind was blowing even stronger and the schoolroom was even darker.

Frances turned round, but the man was no longer there. She was very frightened, but however hard she looked, the man had gone and was no longer to be seen.

At this point, Moira's voice was even more hushed.

Suddenly, Jacqueline heard a cry and then a scream from the bathroom. Terrified she dashed upstairs, but there was no sign of Frances. She ran down to the lounge, and then into the kitchen.

The wind now was so strong they could even hear the sycamore tree outside the chapel moving to such a degree, it sounded like the tree was tapping on the chapel windows, making an eerie noise. Apart from that, the Home, which was normally quite noisy, was as quiet as death itself. The girls instinctively moved closer together, all of them very tense. Moira continued in the same hushed voice,

Jacqueline looked for somewhere to hide, sobbing quietly, desperate and in a blind panic. All of a sudden, the cellar door creaked open.

The girls gasped as just then, suddenly, the door to the boot room crashed open. All the girls screamed, yes even Marlene, and there was a hysterical rush for the door and a race to the comfort and security of the dormitories, where the other girls were talking and laughing, oblivious to what had just occurred. Poor Moira never had the chance to finish the story.

It was a March evening, just after Marlene's birthday, which had been very different owing to a wonderful gift that had appeared on the breakfast table. She had quite forgotten about her birthday and arrived at the refectory on time, a rare occasion in itself! In front of her seat was the most beautiful pot of daffodils and a note telling her that it was a gift from Miss Howkins; she had to read it several times in order to make it real, and also make sure they really were for her, but there they were and Miss Howkins was smiling at her. She put her arms round Miss Howkins and, with tears in her eyes, thanked her profusely. Marlene knew that Miss Howkins would always love Donna best, but she also knew that Miss Howkins must have seen her disappear into the Sisters' garden sometimes to look at the flowers and had said nothing. The gift was her way of saying, *"I know where you go, but it's fine by me!"* This gift was truly special as Marlene was able to keep the daffodils.

However, this was not the end of the story as the daffodils led to an even greater miracle. When the flowers were over, she had asked Sister Maude if she could plant the daffodils in the garden. In reply, Sister Maude led Marlene in to the children's garden, and asked Marlene to find two big stones. When she gave them to Sister Maude, she placed them on a bare piece of earth, about three feet apart, and then told Marlene that this was her garden. Marlene was lost for words; she muttered her thanks as tears of joy streaked her cheeks. In a rare moment of understanding, Sister Maude smiled at her and then disappeared into the Sisters' garden. Marlene ran to Tom to ask him if she could borrow his fork so Tom came over to look at her garden. Under his expert eye, she dug the garden and planted the daffodils and Tom told her that if he had any plants to spare, she could plant them in her garden, with the proviso, that if the garden were not looked after, there would be no more plants.

It was a late March evening at about a quarter to eight and Marlene was going downstairs to wash. As she was going towards the window on the first floor, in the half-light she saw what looked like a nun outside the window waving at her, so Marlene waved back. The gesture was instinctive, and Marlene thought little about it. It wasn't until she was washing that she realised that she had never seen any nun on a ladder, as the nun would have had to be if she could be seen outside the first floor window. Marlene also remembered that all the staff, nuns included, were at supper from half past seven to at least eight o'clock. She wasn't frightened, nor did she leap to any conclusion, ghostly or otherwise. She had seen it and that was enough.

The Home had an extension built later that year, and under that very window, a skeleton was found, one that obviously had not had a Christian burial. Even with this knowledge, Marlene still knew that the experience had not been a frightening one, not nearly as disturbing as having to walk from one end to the other of the Tube or listening to Moira's story. However, she didn't want to tell the girls in case they saw it in the same light as Moira's story - pure fiction. Marlene knew she had seen something important, something she had been privileged to see, but to understand it fully and realise the true significance of it, she would have to wait until she was older.

Chapter 15: A Gentle Death

At the end of chapel one morning, Sister Helena Mary announced that all the girls would stop at school for dinner the Tuesday of the next week as Sister Evelyn had died in her sleep and was to be buried that day. There was a buzz of excited whispering, not, it has to be said, concerning Sister Evelyn's demise, but because of the novelty of school dinners. Marlene was very thoughtful; she wasn't really worried about school dinners, as she knew that whatever was on the menu she would, in all probability, not be able to eat it. The only advantage to be had was that Brian Merril, or someone like him, could be cajoled to eat her dinner as well as his own!

However, she was preoccupied with thoughts of Sister Evelyn's death and subsequent burial. On the Sunday after the death, Marlene had spent most of her time in church looking up the burial service, No one else knew, as she did, the morning service off by heart, so all her responses were in the right place although her mind wasn't on the ordinary Sunday routine, but on the coming funereal service. Marlene had never read the service as up to now she hadn't known anyone who had died and therefore had to be buried, but she thought about it now and was puzzled at the "dust to dust, ashes to ashes," part of the service. If "God made man in his own image" and if Father Hankey was right when he shouted from the pulpit that everyone was born of "sin", then how could they be dust and ashes? As Sister Evelyn was too old to take an active part in the running of the Home, Marlene had met her only on rare occasions, usually when she had been privileged to play with the big dolls in the trunk on the Sisters' landing, but Marlene remembered her as being quite beautiful: she didn't have whiskers like Sister Maude or a very red face and a large body, rather Sister Evelyn was ethereal and her face was smooth, pink and white. Maybe that was how you became when you were very old! Marlene giggled to herself as she thought about Sister Maude becoming like Sister Evelyn. Where would her fatness go?

She played with the idea in her mind, each idea becoming more ridiculous than the last, but eventually returned to the "dust and ashes" problem. Sister Evelyn was quite unlike the ashes from the staffroom fire she had to clean out some mornings as part of her "job", and Sister Evelyn was being buried, not cremated, which after looking it up in the dictionary, she knew meant burnt, but if she wasn't dust or ashes, should she be still alive? Perhaps, just before you died, you suddenly changed into dust and ashes. Yes, that was it. She crept up to the Sisters' landing to try and see if her theory fitted, but the door to Sister Evelyn's room was shut and she heard voices within, so she scuttled downstairs.

Dinner at school proved to be a real experience: boys ate with girls and when it was noticed she was having trouble eating her dinner, Brian Merril predictably asked her if she wanted it and when she shook her head, he scooped it up and swallowed it in seconds. The pupils ate their dinner in the body of the Hall and the teachers sat at the top table on the stage; children were everywhere, and there was a huge cacophony of noise, as if from one mighty voice, rather than from hundreds of individuals.

When they got home at teatime, all the girls were told they must not go into the Sisters' part of the house for any reason, so of course they all adopted their different hiding places, from where each had a different view, so when they met up later, they knew exactly what had happened. Moira, for some time afterwards, kept saying she had seen her ghost, but Marlene, who was absolutely sure that Sister Evelyn was resting peacefully, didn't say anything, although the "dust and ashes" part of the funeral service puzzled her for several years. Indeed, even as an adult, she couldn't understand how anybody could turn to dust and ashes after they were buried, though she supposed that could happen if they'd been buried for centuries!

Chapter 16: Home from Home

Although the year had been momentous, there was yet another milestone just round the corner. The three sisters were summoned by Sister Maude; she talked for a long time about families and, after a few minutes, Marlene had already switched off when, with a start, she realised that Sister Maude had dismissed them. Bille and Dawn were grinning as they made their way to Miss Howkins. Marlene had no idea what was going on, so she had to ask Dawn. She hated doing this, as Dawn always knew everything, and she would put on her "superior elder sister" look. Dawn looked at Marlene in exasperation, but told her that tomorrow all of them were to go on an Easter holiday. Marlene wanted the details, such as where and why and how long for, but Dawn had to confess that the only thing she knew was that they were going to a "family". Miss Howkins was busy sorting through some clothes as they were to have some "new" ones - new to them, that is, but obviously not new from a shop! By bedtime all was prepared for the great adventure.

After breakfast the sisters were told to go to Miss Darnell at 9-30am and then go to Miss Howkins at 10-30am as she was to make sure they were all clean and tidy. When they arrived at the Sewing Room, Miss Darnell showed Marlene a beautiful dress, which she had to try on; it fitted beautifully. Then Dawn tried her "new" dress on and after that it was Bille's turn. Everybody held their breath, waiting for Bille's reaction; Marlene got ready to go and fetch Miss Howkins in case Bille didn't like it, but fortune was on their side. Bille approved!! They all had to have a bath, only taking the allotted two minutes, and then they all had their hair washed; Bille first as she hated having anything done to her hair. She fought all the way and it was some time before she was finished, and Dawn and Marlene could have their turns. Miss Howkins towelled their hair dry, at the same time mentally preparing herself for her biggest task, that of combing and brushing Bille's hair. Miss Howkins and Bille were both on top form and fighting fit and, after half an hour's struggle, the job was done. Dawn and Marlene were easy, so that job was finished in a very short time. Miss Howkins inspected them and when she was satisfied they were all squeaky clean; they were handed their coats and sent to Sister Maude. She inspected them too and then gave Bille Marlene's pristine hanky; it was a source of wonder to the girls and Miss Howkins that Marlene's hanky was never dirty, unless it was tear stained. Marlene hated "lending" her hanky, as she then had a disgusting sticky rag that she had to put up her sleeve, but as Sister Maud had asked her, Marlene had no choice. Sister Maud then decided they must have ribbons for their hair and sent them back to Miss Howkins; Miss Howkins always did the older girls' hair as Miss Guy couldn't reach and more over Marlene didn't altogether like Miss Guy. This idea was completely new to them: ribbons and a "new" dress? But after taking another calculating look at Bille, Miss Howkins decided that, as they were to have an early lunch with Sister Maude, the ribbons could wait until just before they were actually starting this new adventure!.

Marlene immediately began to worry as she knew she could not manage meat, but fortunately it was macaroni cheese, which although she didn't like, she could eat, by swallowing the food with numerous cups of water. When they had finished they had to go back to Miss Howkins for the ribbons. Some of the girls at school had ribbons, but for the sisters it was a first! The only thing they were clear about was there would be yet another battle between Miss Howkins and Bille. Strangely enough that didn't happen, as Bille was so proud that she was to have a ribbon, she completely forgot that this was another opportunity for a battle with her old adversary. Miss Howkins was so surprised that she gave Bille the first choice of colour. This was dangerous, as whichever ribbon Bille chose would be lost forever. Bille chose a lovely red ribbon, Marlene had a green, and so Dawn was left with the blue. Dawn could easily have had a choice, but she was in her "big sister" mood, which meant she was prepared to have what was left over and play the martyr. They all returned to Sister Maude, who inspected them once again, looking particularly hard at Bille, who was so proud of the ribbon that she was perfectly behaved and demure!

They waited on the steps for a few moments until a large black car, driven by her friend Joe, stopped at the nuns' entrance. The three sisters were waiting to see who was getting in this grand car, when to their amazement Sister Maude almost smiled and beckoned them into the taxi; Marlene knew it was a taxi because Joe was driving it so she grinned at Joe, who winked at her and put his fingers to his lips to tell her she shouldn't come and talk to him. Sister Maude sat in the front and even Bille was behaving herself as she was overwhelmed by the magnificence of this adventure. They drove for hours and Bille, seeing there was no one to practice her "black arts" on, fell asleep.

After a long time they drove into a small town and the taxi stopped. Joe opened the door for Sister Maude, and then opened their door; Marlene was just getting out when Sister Maude told Dawn to hurry up. The two of them walked up the small path and rang the bell and, when the door opened, she spent several minutes talking to the lady. Marlene took this opportunity to chat to Joe, but after a minute or so, Sister Maude came back to the car without Dawn and off they went again. Marlene was apprehensive because she didn't know what was happening with Dawn, especially as the front door had closed and Sister Maude was back into the car. Then they stopped again and, after waking Bille, Sister Maude walked her to another front door. Once again the door closed, this time with Bille inside. Now Marlene was on her own and she didn't want to go to a strange house, so when Sister Maude got back into the taxi, Marlene said how kind it was of Sister Maude to bring them, but she'd much rather go home with Dawn and Bille. Sister Maude didn't answer, for they were stopping for the third time. This time it was her turn, and she dreaded it. The front door opened and after Sister Maude had talked to the lady who had opened the door, Sister Maude said goodbye, got into the taxi, and Marlene was alone.

She followed the lady inside and was confronted by two girls who were both younger than her; they all stood and stared at each other. The eldest of the two seemed just a year or so younger, but the youngest girl was about six. The lady told Marlene she was to call her "Auntie Mary", and that the two girls were Jane and Kate. Auntie Mary hurried them to the dining room where a lovely tea was laid out on a white cloth which covered the table. There were flowers on a large cupboard-like piece of furniture that was quite low and had two doors and three drawers; Marlene knew this was a sideboard, as she had seen pictures of them in books she had read at school. The room was light and airy with a large window opening on to a small back garden. After an initial panic as to where she was to sit, and another one wondering what to do with the cloth beside her plate which was encased within a wooden ring, she enjoyed the tea, marvelling at the cake, so unlike the Christmas cake at the Home, which was the only cake they ever had. Marlene half remembered the last time she had cake, at Mrs Richard's house all those years ago, and was lost in the memory of what might have been, sadly comparing her life now to the life that Jane and Kate had and that she too might have had with Mrs Richard.

After tea Jane and Kate asked her questions about where she lived and what her life was like; Marlene just shook her head, and looked at her feet. Auntie Mary admonished the sisters and told them to go out into the garden. Marlene asked what the cloth was for, and Auntie Mary explained how serviettes were used. Then she sat Marlene down, and gently told her she didn't have to answer the girls' questions at the moment, but perhaps she might in the future, when she knew them better. Marlene nodded, but could not understand why anyone would want to know about the Home; after all they had the same routine day in day out, week in week out, month in month out. The only change was when Sister Helena Mary changed the rotas. Kate went to bed soon after tea without a bath, which puzzled Marlene, who had always had a bath before bed. Kate was followed by Jane, who also had a wash. When Auntie Mary told her to go to bed, Marlene asked about a bath and Auntie Mary explained that they normally had just a strip wash in the week, but had a bath on Fridays and Sundays. Marlene's bedroom was Jane's room and she eagerly examined the books on a shelf, but they were all too babyish, so she turned to the books that she'd secretly hidden in her bag before leaving the Home.

The next morning Marlene was woken by music that seemed to be coming from downstairs. She waited awhile as usually she was woken by a bell and wasn't sure what to do, but after waiting a few more minutes, she decided she would get up and creep downstairs; if it wasn't time to get up she could slip into bed again and no one would know. Marlene sidled down the stairs, and peeped in to the room where they had had tea the previous day. Auntie Mary was busy in the adjoining kitchen and she asked if the sound of her vacuum had woken Marlene. Marlene shook her head. She told Marlene to sit at the table while she woke Jane and Kate. Marlene sat at the table looking round for the other table where Auntie Mary would serve from. There wasn't one! She wasn't sure what to do so she waited. After a while Auntie Mary appeared and told her to start. Marlene put her hands together to say "Grace" whilst Auntie Mary was bustling about. The girls appeared and started to open a cereal packet. Marlene sucked in her breath and waited for the inevitable storm as they hadn't said "Grace" and Auntie Mary hadn't said they could start. It didn't come! Auntie Mary returned to the table and, noticing that Marlene hadn't put any cereal in her bowl, passed her the packet after scolding her girls for not making sure she'd had cereal. Marlene ate her cereal and then toast and marmalade. She felt very full, as normally she had the dinner she'd been unable to eat at lunch-time for tea and then sometimes for breakfast the next day, whereas last night she'd had a proper tea.

At lunch time the inevitable happened. It was meat and, try as she might, Marlene couldn't eat it! Eventually, as everyone had finished, Auntie Mary told her she could get down from the table; Marlene asked where she should put her plate so she could continue to try and finish her dinner at teatime. Auntie Mary told her she would deal with it. Teatime came and when the girls sat up to the table, Marlene could not see her dinner plate; she was tempted to say nothing, but it went against her sense of fairness, so she asked where it was. Jane and Kate listened in amazement, but Auntie Mary just told her to eat her tea. Gradually there developed a routine and pattern to the days and, after a few days Marlene had settled in and the week flew by. The girls had many toys and bikes and skates, but soon Marlene had mastered all of them. She would find out many years later that after she went back to the Home, Jane and Kate had asked their mother why Marlene tried out all their toys, learning how to use them in minutes, whereas they still hadn't learned to use them although they'd had them for months. Apparently Auntie Mary had pointed out that they would have their bikes, skates, stilts and all their other toys for a long time whereas Marlene had only had a short time to enjoy them. The girls understood, but even so they still felt a little put out at Marlene learning all the various skills so very quickly.

Auntie Mary was a hairdresser and used to go to clients' houses on her bicycle so all three girls usually followed, running behind her. Her own two girls weren't very happy, as they usually went on their bikes, but only having two bikes for the three of them meant they had to leave their bikes behind. It was quite difficult for Marlene to meet so many people and she longed to be with Dawn and Bille. One day Auntie Mary took them to a big house in the road where Dawn was living; it was Sish Lane, a very funny name Marlene thought. Jane and Kate seemed quite pleased to go and explained to Marlene they were going to "Gargi's"! Marlene was no wiser until Auntie Mary explained she was their Grandmother, and was called "Gargi", because Kate had given her this pet name when she was very young and couldn't say "Grandmother". Marlene was at a loss, as she'd never met a grandmother, well only the grandmother in "Little Red Riding Hood", and she was sure there were no wolves in Stevenage! She asked Jane what a grandmother did, but Jane just laughed and told her mother what Marlene had said. Auntie Mary explained the grandparents' place in the family and told her grandmothers cared for their grandchildren and helped their daughter or son to provide care and extra help when needed.

The house in Sish Lane was much bigger than Auntie Mim's house, but so much smaller than the Home. It was full of china figurines and old furniture and Marlene glimpsed through the window a very large back garden, a little bigger than the Sisters' garden. At the far end she saw several fruit trees, but in the front of the garden were many flowers and shrubs. Marlene was introduced to an elderly lady and asked her if she might go into the garden. When she had gained permission, she wandered round the garden in quiet excitement; she was on her own, as Jane and Kate were not remotely interested in gardens and Auntie Mary had left to do someone else's hair. After a while Jane called to her and said they were going shopping for her grandmother, so all three girls left together and, when they returned to Gargi's house, they found Auntie Mary there doing her mother's hair. Auntie Mary suggested that the three girls should head for home and she would follow later.

The week passed quickly, and as Marlene got up earlier than the girls; this was the time that she and Auntie Mary got to know each other. Auntie Mary told her that she was married to "Uncle" Paul who was in the navy, as she herself had been. She also told Marlene all the mischief she and Uncle Paul had got up to when they were courting, how she would hide underneath his desk when anyone entered his office and other such escapades. Although it took four or five days before she was able to respond (In the Home the girls seldom spoke to the nuns and staff, never initiating conversation and never about things related to their lives), Marlene was eventually able to tell Auntie Mary a little about the Home and her place in it. She spoke about Dawn and Bille and the jobs they had to do, about school and how she changed her name and confided that she didn't really like her new name! Auntie Mary listened carefully, whilst looking as though she was busy sorting laundry.

And so the week came to an end, and Joe's taxi picked them up, this time in reverse order. Bille was even bubblier than she was normally, her black eyes sparkling and telling the others of all the gifts she had received. She informed them that she had three tins of condensed milk and lots of little meringues and much more, ending with a promise that although she couldn't share much with them, they would have a little taste. Dawn spoke a great deal about Auntie Rose, the lady who Dawn lived with and Annie, who was now her friend. Annie was Auntie Rose's eldest girl and was Dawn's age. Bruce was Annie's brother and was the same age as Marlene and Chris was the youngest. Dawn asked about Marlene's "family", but Marlene didn't really have anything to say except that Auntie Mary was very kind.

Marlene was, in some ways, pleased to be back at the Home as she'd missed the most exciting moment of her week. Every Thursday, she would creep down stairs at 7-30pm, whilst the nuns and staff were in supper, and listen outside the door of the older girls' sitting room. There would be some stirring and slightly sinister music and then a voice, in chilling tones, would say: *"Journey in to Space"* and then the music would start again. Marlene never listened to the rest of the program, but spent lots of scary moments imagining what might happen.

Chapter 17: News from Another World

It was rare that news from the outside world penetrated the closed community that was St. Etheldreda's or the Home. The only way they learnt about the country in which they lived was either from the prayers said in chapel, morning or evening, or the prayers in church, or if it was really important, it was mentioned in the daily assemblies at school. As Marlene knew all the services by heart, she seldom actually listened to any of them; however, it would have taken a hermit or a recluse to miss the current events. When old Queen Mary had passed away in a great farewell of black horses wearing black plumes, gun salutes and all the other trappings given to Heads of States at their passing, it had all passed over the girls' heads. Sister Helena-Mary had shown them pictures from "The Scotsman", but few looked at them and fewer even thought about it, forgetting it in less than five minutes. In fact Marlene was far too busy wondering about the terrible school life of "Jane Eyre" to take any notice at all!

However, this latest news from the outside world caught everyone's imagination, even Marlene's. The Princess Elizabeth, the King's eldest daughter, was apparently holidaying in Africa with her husband, Prince Philip, the Duke of Edinburgh, when her father, George the Sixth, had died. It was a case of: "the King is dead, long live the Queen!" The school curriculum was put on hold while various questions were discussed, such as: "How do you think the Queen Mother, as the widow of the late King was now called, might feel now her daughter was not only on the throne, but she would now have to defer to her?" Even Marlene interrupted her reveries about Jane Eyre and took some interest in this important news. Mr Norman had announced in Assembly that each class was to make a class scrapbook of the events unfolding before them and there would be a small prize for the best one. Marlene begged some articles and as many pictures as she could from "The Scotsman" and took them in. Miss Smith, her teacher, gave her a strange look and asked her where she'd obtained them. Marlene said Sister Helena-Mary had given her them and wondered why her contribution was accepted with a certain amount of scepticism. It would be years before she realised that the late 1940's and the early 1950's were a time of great austerity and few families had the money for any newspapers, let alone one as prestigious as "The Scotsman". However, in assembly, her class was awarded the prize for the best scrapbook, but Marlene received nothing as the prize was extra helpings at school dinner, and this was the last thing Marlene wanted!

Mr Norman gave the whole school a day's holiday so they could listen to the funeral service on the radio and although Sister Maud summoned everyone, even Miss Darnell and Miss Digby to the library to hear this historic event, all the girls sat in total boredom, with the exception of Marlene, who had once again used her capacious knickers to read the remaining chapters of "Rebecca". The king's body had apparently lain in state for some days so the "great and the good" could file past, gazing in silence at the remains of the man whose going was to signal the end of an era. Marlene couldn't see the point of looking at a corpse and after finishing "Rebecca" was now reading "Wuthering Heights". The late King's funeral was the finest and grandest in living memory, but the event that was to take place the following June eclipsed anything that had gone on before

June 1953 was the day of the Coronation. All the girls, in common with every school child in the country,was to have a holiday from school.! Sister Maud had arranged for all the girls to watch the Coronation on television. They were to be divided into groups of five and six and each group would go to a different location. Marlene was to be in a group with Miss Howkins and just had to cross the road to Mr. and Mrs. Duncan who ran the baker's shop. Bille was to go with Sister Maud's group. Since the episode in church when Bille was younger, Sister Maud was taking no chances so she always kept Bille close to her. something. As Marlene arrived the baker's wife welcomed them with a large plate of cakes and a glass of orange squash; Marlene looked at the cakes and took ages choosing one. In the end it was between an éclair and a meringue and eventually chose the éclair.

Mrs Duncan then turned on the television set!! Television was a machine where you could actually watch people at the very same time that they were doing something. It was a very new devise and very few people had a set. It was amazing when the commentator said it was ten to eleven and Marlene looking at the clock on the mantelpiece, saw it was indeed ten to eleven. The Queen's carriage could be seen travelling down the Mall and the commentator described the scene as they were watching it! The Queen finally arrived at Westminster Abbey and then a lady was describing the Queen's dress which was encrusted with jewels. Marlene thought the Queen looked very small, even as small as Sister Helena-Mary and she was weighed down by her crown which looked very heavy. When she had to carry the Orb and Sceptre Marlene was worried in case she fell. After all the great and the good returned to Buckingham palace, the Queen and her family came out on to the balcony and everyone in the huge crowd shouted and clapped. Mr Duncan turned the television off and Mrs Duncan brought out more orange squash and another plate of cakes and this time Marlene chose the meringue. It had been an amazing day and even Bille was too tired to cause any mischief on her return.

Summer 1950

Paddling in the pond at the house of Lord Simon Whitbread, Lord Lieutenant of Bedford.

Bille on the far right, with Elsie next to her.

Chapter 18: A Holiday by the Sea

All this was soon forgotten in the "trivial round, the common task", but as spring drifted into summer and the girls with parents were boasting as to where these parents would take them this year, Sister Maude sent for Dawn and Marlene. She told them they were to stay with Sister Helena Mary's mother in Maryport, Cumbria. They both asked about Bille, but were told that Bille was to go somewhere else. Dawn, obviously taking her responsibilities as a big sister very seriously, shouted at Sister Maude and Marlene could only gape. Dawn was always the "Miss-Goody-Two-Shoes", always doing what she was told, and here was Dawn, shouting at Sister Maude for the second time in as many months! After all, reasoned Marlene, did it really matter that Bille wasn't coming with them?

The very next day, even before breakfast, they were woken early and walked to the train station carrying a large bag apiece and with Sister Helena Mary hurrying them along. Dawn had already shouted again at Sister Maude before they set out; apparently she was really very upset that they were leaving Bille behind. Marlene could not understand her at all. After all, as the three of them were in different years, it meant in the general run of things they didn't really talk to each other very much and Marlene couldn't really think of anything she wanted to say to Bille, or even Dawn, come to that, and life was so much easier without Bille!

They arrived at Maryport late that same evening after changing trains at London and then at Carlisle and it was all the sisters could do to stumble into the comfortable beds in a room which was to be their bedroom for the next six weeks. They woke to the sun streaming through the pretty flower-sprigged curtains and the sounds of seagulls wheeling in the deep blue sky. Sister Helena Mary introduced them to her mother, who was a smaller rounder version of herself. It was strange seeing Sister Helena Mary kiss her mother and, even though Marlene could still only see that a box of "Home-made" chocolates was the only good thing that came from having a mother, she was aware of the very strong bond between the two women. Sister Helena Mary took the two girls around the small town, and they were amazed at the number of people who stopped to talk to "our Mary", apparently Sister Helena Mary's "proper" name. They stopped at the harbour, at the Bakery, at the small general shop, the school and lastly at the church and it became obvious that it had cost Sister Helena Mary dear to leave this small town and her mother.

The next day, very early, Marlene could hear voices, so she slipped out of bed and walked on to the landing, where she saw Sister Helena Mary crying and her mother cuddling her and kissing her. Marlene would normally have rushed downstairs to find out what was going on, but on this occasion she went thoughtfully back to the bedroom, peering out the window, and waving when Sister Helena Mary turned away from the house. She went downstairs and found Mrs Gibson wiping her eyes. Marlene asked why Sister Helena Mary had to go away from all her family and friends and Mrs Gibson told her it was God's will, but Marlene couldn't understand how any person, God or anyone, could make families live apart. Mrs Gibson just smiled in a tired sort of way and said she'd understand some day, and did she want real Scottish porridge for breakfast. Marlene told her about Mrs Richards and that she could have had a family, but Sister Maude hadn't let her. Did this mean that Sister Maude was a sort of God? Mrs Gibson just said her porridge was getting cold and asked her to wake her sister.

This was the start of an idyllic time for the two girls. They "swam" in the sea, lying flat on the sand like starfish, the sea just covering their bodies, as that was how you apparently swam. However, they both worried about Bille. It was not because they were close, as everything in the Home was run in chronological order and days often passed without the three sisters speaking to one another, but they always knew where each other was and, if they really wanted to see one another which was unlikely, they could within minutes. Now they were parted, and Marlene was able to see in a small way why Dawn had got upset! This was the first time since they were sent to the Home they'd been parted from Bille and for Marlene it was the first time in her life. Both of them were concerned about Bille, as neither of them could understand why they had been sent away, but because they were only children, and particularly "Home kids" who never knew the "whys and wherefores" and were used to doing what they were told without querying it, it didn't prey on their minds.

They soon began to find an order to the summer days. On Sunday they went to church and after church they stopped at the paper man to buy Mrs. Gibson "The Scotsman". Marlene remembered that far off "Stir up" Sunday, when four-year-old Bille had led her own "revolution" against the pious nuns and she had questioned in her mind whether Sister Helena Mary should be buying the same paper every Sunday morning. Perhaps now, six years later, her question would be answered She asked Mrs. Gibson how it was that Sister Helena Mary was able to buy "The Scotsman" every week, when all nuns had to take the vow of poverty; after all, the three knots on their girdle were a constant reminder of their sacred vows. Mrs. Gibson smiled and told her that there was so little she could do for Sister Helena Mary, or "our Mary", as Mrs. Gibson called her, and it was she who provided the money for the paper. Mrs Gibson added she was so pleased to do it because, in a strange way, she felt nearer her daughter, knowing that they both read the same paper. Marlene wondered aloud whether it was cheating; after all no money meant no money and no material goods must mean nothing, not even papers. Mrs. Gibson told her she had to write to the Reverend Mother to get permission and it was granted, so Sister Helena Mary had her paper every week. Marlene felt a glow of satisfaction as that problem was now solved. She loved the way life seemed to solve all problems in time and those that could not be solved, well, you just put them out of your mind and went on to meet the next thing; at least, that was the theory! She also started to appreciate the huge demands made on all the families of nuns, but more so on Mrs Gibson, as Sister Helena

Mary was an only child and her husband had died in the war. The idea that God had now replaced their human family, sounded good, but the reality was devastating.

On Monday Mrs. Gibson did the washing and Dawn and Marlene took turns to crank the mangle, checking that the clothes and bed sheets were not tangled but were able to go through the mangle easily. Because Mrs Gibson lived by the sea, and it was usually quite windy, clothes were dried in a few hours. Tuesday, Mrs. Gibson went to see her friend and Marlene and Dawn played in the garden. It wasn't a big garden, but it felt good. Mrs Gibson's friend hadn't a husband either and the two old friends would gossip away the time while the girls drank tea and ate Mrs. Ferguson's home-made ginger biscuits. Wednesday was market day, and Marlene and Dawn were allowed to walk round the market by themselves and although they couldn't buy anything, because they didn't expect it, it didn't matter. Mrs. Gibson bought meat and vegetables, fruit and eggs and the girls were laden with shopping on their way back. Thursday they sometimes went for a picnic by the sea and this was the day the girls liked the best, though in fact every day was special. Friday they went to the fish man; they had to go quite early in the morning and they never knew what they would buy because it depended on what Mr. Mackay had caught that morning. The girls had never been shopping and the idea that what you bought depended on what was caught from the sea that very morning delighted Marlene and satisfied her need to "make things work", to fit in with nature and the natural way of things

The summer passed by in a haze of hot lazy days, and dreamless nights. They woke to the sound of gulls wheeling past their window that looked out to the sea and went to bed, rocked by the sounds of the waves. All too soon Marlene and Dawn were back in Bedford and their idyllic holiday was but a dream.

MARYPORT 1950

Dawn and Marlene "swimming" at Maryport

Dawn in the Garden at Maryport

Chapter 19: Climbing to the Heights and Depths

It was late summer on a Saturday morning and the weather was still warm. All the girls seemed to be milling around the back garden, their jobs done for the time being, and they were enjoying their free time. Saturday afternoons were spent in a "crocodile" being walked to the Golf Club or along Clapham Road to the sports field. Marlene just wanted to do her garden, but she knew that she wouldn't be allowed to, as Moira in particular hated anyone doing anything which she couldn't do. Even if she herself had no interest in it, she couldn't stand anyone not hanging on her every word, so Marlene wandered over to where the others were. She soon discovered that there were only about a dozen of the girls there: Bille's gang, Dawn, Moira. Ethel, Dilly and a few others were all by the swing. Moira had decided they would all climb the wall and see into Mr. Piper's garden. Mr Piper kept the bookshop across the road and wouldn't allow any of the girls, or any children for that matter, to go into the shop.

Marlene tried to slink away, as she knew she was no good at climbing or running; she couldn't seem to be able to get enough breath and then she'd panic at the thought that everyone was laughing at her. However, Moira suddenly shouted her name and said Marlene would be able to climb the wall easily. Marlene looked for help from Dawn, but Dawn had switched off her "older sister" role and was oblivious to Marlene's distress. Marlene stuttered her refusals, but Moira seized her and with some of the other girls began pushing Marlene up the wall. Dawn was laughing with all the others and, as Marlene's face was to the wall, no one could see it wasn't a game, except Moira. Suddenly Marlene felt her bladder give and the girls' laughter turned to disgust as the urine splashed on to their hands. Marlene ran and ran, inside, up the stairs in absolute shame; she knew she would never live this down. Suddenly she heard Dawn calling her; she was very quiet, hoping Dawn would give up looking for her and return to the others. But no, Dawn came and found her. Dawn cuddled her and said no-one was laughing at her and it was all her, Dawn's, fault, for not looking out for her and anyway it was a stupid game, as everyone knew Marlene never had enough breath for anything like that. Dawn persuaded her to come back downstairs and, indeed, it was true, no one mentioned it again.

There seemed to be more bees this year as Marlene's daily count was up noticeably. Although she had never been stung by a bee nor a wasp, not even when she stroked them, she was doing handstands with the other girls in the Sisters' garden, and unfortunately placed one of her hands on a bee who was quietly going about its business; the inevitable happened, but though her hand was sore, Marlene felt more upset as the bee was dead. Bille was also stung by a bee on her shoulder, and within minutes, her neck swelled so it was on a level with her shoulders, and both eyes were as black as if she had been in a prize fight!! She couldn't talk and was rushed to hospital. Bille was diagnosed with a fatal allergy to bee and wasp stings and Dawn too was found to be allergic many years later.. Bille lived in Northern Ireland from the age of 18 and hearing of her allergy, the medical profession advised her to say five "Hail Mary's" if she was stung. Dawn, who emigrated to Australia, was given some serum to carry with her in the event of her being stung. The difference in values and protocol between the two counties could not have been clearer!

Several weeks later Marlene crept upstairs for a quiet read. She had started "Little Women", but it was difficult to find a spot where she wouldn't be interrupted. As she walked through Moira's, Dawn's and Ethel's little dormitory, she heard Dawn whisper her name. She looked over the Sisters' stairs and then back where she had come from, but couldn't see her sister. Then she heard a soft giggle and Dawn called her name again. Dawn's head suddenly appeared through the window. It was a sort of dormer window with a small landing outside that was a third of the way up the roof. Marlene looked incredulously and Dawn laughed and beckoned to her to follow out the window.

Ethel and Moira were there too and now, Dawn and Ethel were going to climb the steep pitched roof. Marlene pleaded with them, but the two of them were determined. Marlene followed at a distance as Dawn and Ethel climbed to the top; Dawn was giving a running commentary on who they could see: Mr. Piper, Sister Eleanor, Maggie, but the commentary was cut short by a loud tortured scream. It was Maggie who had just looked up and seen them and before the two could vanish over the apex of the roof, Sister Maud, Sister Helena-Mary and Miss Howkins had joined Maggie in the front garden. Within seconds and before they could clamber down the roof and into the bedroom, Miss Howkins was there, ordering them downstairs to await their fate. They all lined up outside Sister Maud's office and were beaten, but instead of sending them off one by one, Sister Maud made them all wait outside while she, Sister Helena-Mary and Miss Howkins held a long consultation. Eventually the girls were ordered back inside the office and were told that bars would be fixed to all the bedroom windows and that they would have to all pay seven shillings and sixpence out of their pocket money which would probably take at least a year! As Marlene never seemed to have any pocket money it was immaterial to her, but Ethel, Moira and Dawn were very upset.

On the following Monday, Sister Maud was as good as her word and locks appeared at all the windows; Marlene still didn't get any pocket money, which in any case had been stopped as far back as she could remember because she couldn't eat her dinner, but Dawn and the others suffered. However the kudos they got from the other girls more than made up for it and it went down in the annals of St Etheldreda's as a real epic adventure. Marlene was happy, as this adventure outshone the humiliation she had suffered because of the fiasco of the wall!

The Home 1952

1st row: 1st left, Bille

2nd row: 1st left, Donna. Next to Donna one of the twins.

3rd row: 3rd row 2nd left, Patsy, and next to her Dilly; 4th left, Marlene, next to her Dawn and then, Moira

4th row: 1st left, Elsie and next to her Ethel.

Chapter 20: Away Again To The Seaside

It was early November and at school Marlene's class had to sit an exam; they all had to sit in the hall and they were given a question paper. Many of her class were very worried, and particularly one of Marlene's friends. She didn't have a best friend, all that was over since Barbara, but Janet who she sat next to in class was particularly concerned about the outcome of the exam. She told Marlene that her Mum and Dad were going to buy her a new bike if she passed, but Marlene just sat and completed the paper without a thought as to what the consequences would be. The next day at school some of the girls were crying and telling her that their parents had said it was the most important thing they would ever have to do! They were going over their papers in their heads, with the exception of Marlene and a boy called Philip Rogers. Philip had made quite an impression on Marlene, but she couldn't have said why: perhaps it was because he never made fun of her, though to be fair, most of the class didn't now. Perhaps it was because he, like Marlene, usually knew the answers in class, but unlike Brian Merril, her age-old enemy from Infants School, he didn't jump up and down and yell answers that were generally wrong!

Christmas came and went and on a chill January day, while they were still on holiday, they were again summoned to Sister Maud's office. This time, Bille was summoned too. It was odd that when they returned to the Home and were reunited with their sister once again, they could find little to say to her. Marlene wasn't even absolutely sure which dormitory Bille was in, but thought it must be that as long as Bille was with them, they didn't need to converse. Sister Maude told them that the very next day all three of them were to go away. They were to go to the seaside again, but this time, to Broadstairs in Kent. Marlene and Dawn lost no time in telling Bille what a wonderful time they would have. They described the market, the fish-man, the dairy, hearing the waves crashing on the shore while lying in bed, and all the other exciting features of a seaside holiday. They also warned Bille not to spoil it and to **behave**!

Marlene, never a good sleeper, was awake all night, smiling in the dark and going over all the exciting things they would do and see. She knew they would not be able to "swim" as the weather was so cold, but they could do all the other exciting things a seaside holiday promised. The three sisters were up with the lark; Marlene could never work out why the bird mentioned was a lark, when it was really the dawn chorus. All through breakfast the sisters kept glancing at each other, their faces wreathed with smiles, but the meal seemed interminable. At last it came to an end, and after chapel the three girls went at once to Miss Howkins, who washed their hair and told them to change into the clothes she'd laid on their beds. They got ready quickly and then Miss Howkins dried their hair and gave them ribbons to put on. Marlene and Dawn scowled at Bille to remind her to be good, but for once she was sweetness itself and they hurried to the Sisters' hall. It was Sister Maude who was going to accompany them, and although the three girls would rather have had Sister Helena Mary as a companion, they were all too excited to worry about such a small detail.

Joe took them to the station and, as the train was waiting, they boarded quickly. Bille had only been on a train once when she was two when she first came to the Home and kept running from one window to another. As Dawn was in "big sister" mode, she was no fun, so Marlene buried herself in her book, which had travelled in her knickers in case Sister Maude recognised the book as one that should have been in the library and confiscated it. However Sister Maude was too busy muttering to herself while reading from her prayer book.

Their first glimpse of Broadstairs from the taxi window could not have been any more different from the approach to Maryport. They couldn't see the sea and the town looked cold and forbidding. Marlene and Dawn hastily explained to Bille, who was becoming increasingly agitated, that once they saw the sea, it would be exactly as they had described it. The taxi made its way round the rain-splashed roads, and eventually stopped at a large house, almost as big as St. Etheldreda's. Sister Maude hurried them inside, where they were met by a member of staff who looked even crosser than Sister Maude. They were taken to a relatively small bedroom with three beds in it and told this was to be their bedroom. They were also told to wash and get into bed straight away. A glance at Bille's face told them that if things did not get better, Bille was going to make her feelings felt, but that would be tomorrow and, worn out by the journey, all three of them slept soundly.

They were roughly shaken awake. With no bell to wake them, or at least not one they could hear, they had overslept and were already judged and found wanting! And so began a miserable existence. They knew nobody and they were not allowed to talk at mealtimes as one of the staff read long passages from the Bible. They were used to going to chapel after breakfast, but as there was no school to go to, the service went on and on. Their jobs which in the Home had taken half an hour every morning and evening, were stretched to take well over an hour and when finished they had to wait until their work had been inspected before they were allowed to go and read for half an hour: Marlene was glad she had taken a book from the Home, as the choice of books seemed more suited to a Victorian schoolroom and seemed generally about places in other countries. They found little to interest them and also missed the Home, especially Bille, who found little solace in reading, and in the Home had a large "gang" to see to her every need. Here there was no one.

Dinner was served and Marlene's heart sank as she knew she couldn't eat it and, with no school, she was made to stay there for the next two hours. After that she still couldn't finish it and knew what would happen next, so she was not surprised when at tea time and breakfast time the next morning she was faced with the plate of cold and congealed food, which, although there was less on her plate than there was at lunch time, she still couldn't finish.

In the afternoon, the girls spent two hours singing hymns, a session which Marlene missed every day as she was still trying to eat her dinner. Just before tea they were taken for a walk by the seaside. Dawn and Marlene lost no time in telling Bille all she could look forward to: the sea birds and the boats and the beach itself with sand as far as the eye could see. They had to go everywhere in "crocodile" so were not allowed to walk together, but they managed to whisper to Bille that, once they were on the beach, they would be allowed to run and play with each other. As it was just after Christmas, the weather was very cloudy and bitterly cold, and when they got on to the beach, they could not see any sand, just big rocks and greasy sea weed. Since they were still in their crocodile, Marlene and Dawn had no way to soften the blow, and true to form, Bille started to rebel. She pulled out of the crocodile and started to run towards the sea, but kind Miss Howkins wasn't there, so Bille had to be pulled away forcibly and frog-marched back to the house by a member of staff. That set the pattern of the rest of the time they spent at Broadstairs!

Over the next four weeks or so the staff seemed to be always telling Bille off and making her spend long hours on her own, either sitting outside the staff quarters or banished to their bedroom. To Marlene and Dawn this would have been heaven, as they were both inveterate bookworms, reading several books a week, but Bille did not have this outlet, and so became more and more morose and depressed. She lost the mischievous sparkle in her black eyes, and instead of going at her usual breakneck speed, she now moved at a snail's pace. Bille grew ever more listless and Dawn and Marlene grew more anxious with each passing day. They talked and worried about her until Marlene suggested Dawn talk to the staff: "After all, you are the eldest!" Dawn reluctantly agreed and, after they had discussed many ideas, went off to try and discover why the staff were giving Bille such a hard time. Dawn reappeared quite quickly, telling Marlene they denied they'd treated Bille any differently, so the sisters decided they'd stay with Bille every minute of the remaining days.

The days dragged by. Bille seldom had a good night's sleep so Marlene, who, from years of lying awake listening to the night noises, slept very badly, often crept into bed with her little sister to cuddle and whisper to her, reminding her of all the fun she had in the Home and told her again and again that they'd be going home very soon. So with Marlene doing the night shift and Dawn watching over her in the daytime, they managed to keep Bille going through the long weeks until the eagerly awaited news came: they were going back!

The effect this news had on Bille was little short of a miracle as the day before they were due to return was payback time! Big time! Bille was more than back to normal. Put simply, she gave the staff hell, but as they were leaving the next day there was little the staff could do about it. On the seaside walk, long acquaintance with the very docile Bille had made the staff sloppy and they'd quite forgotten the Bille who had made things so difficult when she first arrived. Bille, knowing this, had made a plan; she ran into the sea, ,making sure she was in far enough to make anyone trying to get her back extremely wet!! She absolutely refused to come out and led the staff a merry and very wet dance until one of the staff finally caught her.

Teatime was a riot, with Bille pretending to be sick and making the most horrible noises that had all the other girls in hysterics. She was sent to bed early, but kept coming downstairs, causing even more laughter and confusion. Marlene and Dawn were delighted to see Bille back to normal and even Dawn, who would normally perform the big sister act, hadn't the heart to remonstrate with her. The journey home passed without incident, and as Bille was so pleased to be going home, she forgot to annoy Sister Maud, who had come to collect them. The two older sisters would only understand why Bille was treated so badly many years later: they had never thought that the colour of Bille's skin was any different than anyone else's, never seen her as black, or, if not exactly black, then noticeably dark skinned. She was just their sister Bille, and in the Home was treated the same as everyone else.

21: A Visit From "God" and Another Weapon in her Armoury Against Bullies

One dark February day in the half term holidays, Marlene was summoned to Sister Maude's office after she'd seen Miss Howkins and changed her clothes. She was cleaning the stairs at the time, but dutifully went to find Miss Howkins. After she'd washed and changed and brushed her hair, Marlene went to find Dawn, as she couldn't imagine what Sister Maud wanted: she didn't think she'd done anything wrong. Marlene asked her why she'd been summoned, but Dawn had to confess she didn't know. It was such a rare occasion for Dawn to admit to not knowing something that Marlene began to get quite worried. However, she made her way to the office and after knocking and being ordered to come in, found Sister Maud with a very tall man in a purple cassock with a large gold coloured cross round his neck.

Sister Maud told her that as Dawn was being confirmed in a few weeks, she had written to the Bishop asking him if Marlene could be confirmed at the same time. The Bishop was intrigued by this request as the Church's advice was that candidates for confirmation should be of an age to understand what confirmation meant and also be adult enough to make the very serious commitment to God. Twelve or thirteen was the very earliest age at that the Bishop had confirmed anyone, with fourteen or fifteen being the optimum. He had told Sister Maud this and, to be fair to Sister Maud, until Dawn, who was twelve, she had never put a candidate forward who was under thirteen. However, this time Sister Maud had insisted that he come and see this precocious ten year old child. He started the interview, because that was what it was, by asking her about herself and what she liked to do in her free time. Marlene told him about the books she had read and the garden she was working on. Sister Maud explained that Marlene was the only child with a garden and the Bishop nodded. He asked her about some of the books she had read recently and asked where she got the books from, "from the library, perhaps?"

There was a long silence until Sister Maud prompted him to consider Marlene's knowledge and understanding of the Church. He then asked Marlene about the creed which she was able to recite from start to finish, the Bible, her preoccupation with the chapel and her general knowledge about Christianity generally. After long minutes had passed he was finally satisfied and asked Marlene if she would like to be confirmed. Marlene really had no opinion but, as she looked at Sister Maud, she saw it mattered very much to her, so she nodded; whereupon the Bishop stood up, kissed her on the forehead and, whilst signing her with the sign of the Holy Cross, said "Bless you, my child."

Dawn was waiting in the corridor that connected the Sisters' rooms to the girls' side of the house, and, as Marlene came down the corridor, she said she'd been waiting ages and wanted to know if Marlene was in trouble. The thought of her being in trouble was laughable as, if it wasn't for her eating problems and taking books from the Sisters' library without asking, Marlene never really did anything to invite trouble. She just muttered the gist of it, and Dawn and Marlene soon forgot all about it.

Now Marlene was initiated into the mysteries of confession, or at least her first confession. As the girls were only allowed out for school and "wholesome" walks always in "crocodile", it was difficult to imagine what they possibly could have to confess, but this worried Marlene not at all. Sister Maud had said she would look at the lists of "sins" if the girls were not sure. However Marlene was very sure: after all, she had the Bible! Very soon she had a comprehensive list which read thus:

I have lied.

I have cheated.

I have bullied Bille (repeated 20 times with different names).

I have coveted from Bille_(repeated 20 times with different names).

I have coveted from the Sister Maud (although the nuns had nothing).

I have coveted from Sister Eleanor (repeated to name all the nuns).

I have coveted from my neighbour (whom she never spoke to and didn't know anyway).

I have committed adultery with Bille(repeated 20 times with any name).

I have murdered Bille's dreams (repeated 20 times with different names).

I have not honoured my father (she didn't have one as far as she knew!)

I have not honoured my mother (ditto).

I have been gluttonous (even though she couldn't eat the meagre food she was given).

I have been slothful (she had to do the work set for her).

I have not kept the Sabbath (she didn't have an option).

I have trespassed on the 4th of January. (She was guilty of going into the Sister's garden, repeated with another 12 dates.)

I have blasphemed (taken the Lord's name in vain).

She was very proud of her "sin list", especially when Dawn came and asked her how many she had, as she could only find eight. Marlene proudly said she had 106, and she would give Dawn another ten, but kept all the good ones a secret.

The evening came when they had to go to church to confess. Marlene proudly carried her list, her very long list. It was 6-30pm and quite dark in the enormous church. They were the only ones there, except for the bats that chattered and dive-bombed them. Marlene was fascinated, but she could tell Dawn was uneasy, even though she was in "big sister mode" and couldn't show it! Dawn had lost face over THE LIST, so couldn't afford to look vulnerable. The priest, Father Court, was sitting in the Lady Chapel and Dawn was called first; Sister Maud had decreed the order and had made Dawn go first as she could show Marlene how to do it. Dawn was soon done, but Marlene hadn't time to quiz her, before she was called.

Marlene knelt down where Father Court indicated. He blessed her and asked her for her confession. There was a strange smell emanating from the priest, not unpleasant, but very different, almost, but not quite, a Christmas pudding smell. Marlene very proudly started her list. She knew she had to speak clearly, but she also spoke loudly, as she wasn't sure if the priest suffered from deafness. After the first dozen or so, she heard a peculiar sound, and then a fit of coughing from Father Court. Marlene stopped and asked if she was going too quickly. The priest was unable to talk properly, but waved his hand for her to continue. It was a good fifteen minutes later when Marlene at last finished her list, whereupon Father Court stood up and hurried into the vestry, where more noises and what sounded like coughing were heard for another five minutes or so. Marlene still knelt and waited until he came back.

On his return he asked her to give him her list, and if she had made her list "prayerfully" and if she had indeed committed all those sins. Marlene said she had read the Bible's Ten Commandments and had taken a very long time thinking about it in the chapel! She then told Father Court how much she loved being in the chapel, telling him about the lime trees and the stained glass windows. She was just starting on the Saints in the windows when he cut her short, blessed her and told her that God had forgiven her sins. "All of them!" he emphasized and then another strange coughing fit came over him and he gestured her to leave, while he almost ran back into the vestry.

Dawn couldn't understand what had been going on as she'd been watching Father Court leave and come back and then leave again and had heard all the strange noises. Marlene felt she must speak to Sister Maud in case Father Court was really ill. She told her about the coughing and Father Court's apparent discomfort and then explained, rather proudly, that she did have 106 sins on her list, and so perhaps he was tired. At this point Sister Maud asked her for her list, but Marlene said perhaps Father Court had forgotten to hand it back after the confession was finished. Strangely, he hadn't asked Dawn for hers. Sister Maud said "hmm" and dismissed her, reminding her she would have to go to confession every other week. Marlene was delighted. The date for their Confirmation came nearer and nearer and the best part was they were all going to wear "new" clothes, not new, of course, but lovely different ones which they just had for the day. There were four candidates from the Home and no one realised one of them had special dispensation. Marlene didn't feel any different, and life went on as before except she saw the bats twice a month, and was much in demand as a "confession list" writer, which gave the bullies another reason to leave her alone.

Chapter 22: Auntie Mary Plays Detective

In the Easter holidays the three sisters were once more off to Stevenage. This time they were to catch the bus from Bedford to Hitchin, and they would be met there to take a further bus to Stevenage. They walked to the bus station accompanied by Sister Eleanor. Bille was so excited about going on a bus ride on their own, she quite forgot to give poor Sister Eleanor a difficult time, which was just as well as Sister Eleanor was at her fussiest. When they arrived at the bus station, they had to wait a few moments for the bus to arrive. Bille was getting more and more difficult when, in answer to Sister Eleanor's' prayers, the bus came just in the nick of time. The three sisters piled in and Sister Eleanor paid the conductor and then had a long whispered conversation with him, with many a meaningful glance at Bille. At last the bus was on its way; Dawn started to give a long "elder sister" speech to Bille, but Bille was looking out of the window, entranced by the countryside, villages and towns they were passing through. She kept up a running commentary to Dawn, knowing it was no use speaking to Marlene who was already deep into a book. She'd smuggled out a couple of new ones and while the others were settling down, she was busy rescuing them from the legs of her capacious knickers. Dawn noticed this and was just going to do her "elder sister bit", when she glanced at Marlene's face and thought better of it.

The journey was soon over and looking out of the bus window as it drove into Hitchin, Marlene saw Auntie Mary. She fiercely warned Bille of the direst consequences - at least "death and damnation" - if she were to "play up", as she was sure Auntie Mary would decide she wanted nothing to do with anyone who had a sister like Bille! Bille also glanced at Marlene's face and decided that she didn't really want to misbehave. After all, in just a short time, she would have several tins of condensed milk and as many sweeties as she could eat. The bus to Stevenage was waiting, so they quickly climbed aboard: Jane was with Auntie Mary, but Kate had stayed with "Gaga". Soon the group of five were at Stevenage, where they picked up Kate, dropped Dawn off, and then Bille. Eventually Marlene, Auntie Mary, Jane and Kate arrived home.

The week passed quickly, but Marlene noticed Auntie Mary kept looking at her when she was trying to eat her dinner. Auntie Mary asked her why she couldn't eat her meat, but Marlene didn't know; she just knew it "wouldn't go down". Auntie Mary then asked her why she drank so much water, but Marlene had been doing it so long she didn't have an answer and, as she wanted to try out some new roller skates that Jane had, didn't really give the matter a great deal of thought. Auntie Mary said no more, so Marlene got down from the table and "borrowed" the skates, mastering them in an afternoon; Jane was relieved that Marlene had learnt to skate so quickly as now she could play with them. Marlene often trawled through Jane's books, but found them too babyish, which was why she had already visited the Sisters' Library, loading up her commodious knickers so she always had a store of books to read.

Towards the end of the week, Auntie Mary told her that, although they had arranged that Dawn's "Auntie Rose" would take them to Hitchin to put them on the bus to Bedford, she was now going the whole journey with them as she wanted a word with Sister Maud. Marlene's heart sank! She tried to think what it was she had done wrong. On the last night Marlene asked if she could go to bed after tea. Auntie Mary was puzzled, as usually the three girls wanted to stay up later, but she gave her permission and Marlene went up to her bedroom. In the privacy of the room, she wrote down all she had done that week in an attempt to discover what had prompted Auntie Mary's decision not to have her to stay anymore, for she was convinced that was what Auntie Mary wanted to see Sister Maud about. Marlene came up with nothing, but then it occurred to her that it was the same reason the girls from the High School held their noses when they passed any of the Home girls and pushed them off the pavement: everyone knew the Home girls were smelly and dirty and that's why they were called "dirty smelly Home girls". How could she have believed that anyone with a lovely house and lovely children with lots of new clothes and exciting toys would want them to live with anyone like her?

Marlene thought she ought to say thank-you to Auntie Mary, and tell her she understood, but couldn't think of the words to use. She heard Kate come up to bed and, it seemed to her, a long while later that Jane came up too. Marlene felt that she should talk to Auntie Mary now, while Jane and Kate were in bed, so if things didn't go well she wouldn't have an audience. She crept downstairs, clutching her tear-stained hanky. Auntie Mary was sitting in an armchair, writing, probably a letter to Uncle Paul who was still in the navy. She looked up when Marlene came in, but didn't seem surprised. Marlene stuttered out the apology, saying how sorry she was, though what for she didn't know, and how much she'd loved coming. Auntie Mary was silent for some time, but then she came over to her and gave her a hug. In the Home the girls were never hugged and kissed, and Auntie Mary had never done it before, so this was unusual in itself, but then Auntie Mary said of course Marlene could come again and the reason she needed to speak to Sister Maude was entirely different. Auntie Mary added that, as it was to be an adult conversation, she couldn't tell Marlene about it, but she should know that Marlene had done nothing wrong, and she must go to bed now and get a good night's rest.

The next day, after they had picked up Dawn and Bille, they caught the bus to Hitchin. Bille was laden with tins of condensed milk and sweeties, which as usual she declined to offer to her sisters. Jane and Kate had been dropped off at Gaga's house, so it was just Auntie Mary and the three sisters. Marlene had already given Bille the "look" to warn her not to get into any mischief, so the bus ride passed without incident. They arrived in Hitchen and quickly made their way to the bus stop for the last leg of their journey. The bus arrived in minutes and with Marlene sitting with Auntie Mary and Dawn, lost in a new book, "borrowed" from Marlene, the journey passed without incident. Bille was also quiet for now, as she was gobbling sweets as fast as she could, reasoning the less she had when they arrived at the "Home", the fewer she'd have to share. Even though Bille wasn't one to be bullied or cajoled into anything resembling "fair play", she very, very occasionally had an attack of conscience, which fortunately never lasted long enough to trouble her. They were back in Bedford within a very short time and were climbing the steps of the Sisters' front door.

Sister Maud herself answered the door and, after looking hard at Marlene, showed Auntie Mary into her office. Marlene hurriedly thanked her and said goodbye and joined her sisters as they ran into the school room. After a short while, Marlene went upstairs to watch Auntie Mary leave, trying to see if she was angry, but Auntie Mary gave no clue,as to what the "adult" talk was about. as she walked quickly down the drive

After this her life seemed to change: she felt Sister Maud, the other nuns and Miss Howkins staring at her, particularly at mealtimes. A few days later Marlene was summoned to Sister Maud's office and this time the Doctor was there. He peered up her nose, then got out a little torch and shone that up her nose too. He said "Hmm," put his torch away and nodded at Sister Maud. Marlene was dismissed and went to find Dawn, who knew nothing!

Something was wrong: Marlene no longer had to eat her dinner cold at tea time, and then again cold at breakfast. She was getting increasingly annoyed as Sister Maud, Sister Helena-Mary and even Miss Howkins had taken to peering up her nose, but when her teachers at school started to do it, she'd had enough. Marlene went to talk to Dawn, who only knew Marlene might have to go to hospital. In the end she asked Miss Howkins who told her that when she was three, she'd had her adenoids out and a swab had been left in her nose, so she couldn't eat and breathe. Miss Howkins also told her that, because of this, she couldn't eat meat quickly which was why she had so many problems with eating her dinners. Marlene had no fears about the impending hospital visit: she had been so institutionalised that if that was what Sister Maud had decided, then that was what she must do. All things considered if it meant she was no longer to be punished for not being able to eat her dinners, then that was a very good thing. Another plus was that she might even be allowed some of her pocket money, but, as she couldn't remember a time when she'd had money, she had no idea what to spend it on!

Chapter 23: A Prolonged Stay in Hospital

A very short time later Marlene went into hospital. She was to have tests for a couple of days, and then would have her operation. The next day Sister Helena-Mary came to visit her, but had to talk to the Matron first. Sister Helena-Mary and Matron were standing quite near her bed, and so she heard Sister Helena-Mary ask if the operation would affect her brain. Marlene had never heard adults discussing her before, so she listened intently. The Matron shook her head, and then asked Sister Helena-Mary why she'd asked such an odd question. The nun explained that Marlene apparently had achieved the highest marks in the mock eleven plus exam, apparently scoring 99%, which was the highest score ever recorded, and so she was to be sent to the High School. Sister Helena-Mary also was told that Marlene should be out in a week. Marlene was so quiet during the visit that Sister Helena-Mary soon left, leaving Marlene to her thoughts. Marlene didn't know what to do: the High School was sited close to the Home and the girls who attended the school took great delight in bullying the "Dirty Smelly Home Kids". Many a time she had been pushed off the pavement by the girls with their strange hats and silly voices and now she was to go to the same school! She knew she couldn't do it; she knew she wouldn't have the right clothes. Even at their infant and junior schools they were sometimes called names. But the High School! What was she to do?

The operation came and went, but instead of getting back to normal, Marlene seemed to go into a decline. She seldom talked, seldom ate and seldom slept. The hospital was concerned and put her on a course of penicillin, administered by injections in her bottom which rapidly became very bruised. Sister Helena-Mary and Miss Howkins came regularly and asked Marlene countless times if there was anything the matter. Marlene longed to confide in Miss Howkins but, as she'd never confided in anyone since Doreen, she just didn't know how. A week stretched into two, then three and Marlene still couldn't think what she was to do. She kept having nightmares in which she was in the High School changing rooms, wearing second-hand, or even third- or fourth-hand clothes all of which were patently not the High School uniform; in the nightmares she was subjected to cruel laughter and bullying that she knew she couldn't run away from. After three and a half weeks had passed, the answer came to her: she would go into the exam room and answer every question incorrectly. When Marlene knew the answer she would write down the opposite. She immediately began to get better and, after four weeks in hospital, she was finally well enough to go home. There were no after effects except she found out for the first time what a horrid thing a runny nose was and, as a consequence, never had a clean hanky again.

The morning of the exam came and Marlene duly put her plan into action. When the results were announced, she was to go to the Harpur Central School with all the other girls from the Home and, as her plan had been so successful, she didn't even make the top class, but was put in the "B" class along with Rosie and some of her class mates from the Junior School, including her friend Janet. Now, although it would not be true to say she was looking forward to her new school, at least she wouldn't have nightmares about it.

Marlene found herself lying on the floor! Her foot had slipped on the stairs as she was getting ready for bed. It soon became clear that her right foot was damaged; she called out, but there was no reply so she made her way down two flights of stairs and across two landings, but hopping and crawling. Marlene banged on St. Andrew's door and the bigger girls came out. It was clear to everyone that Marlene had really hurt herself as her right foot was now twice as large as her left.. The commotion brought Miss Howkins to the scene, followed by Sister Maud. A taxi was called and took her and Sister Maud to the hospital.

When the Dr. examined her foot, he explained that there was no x-ray operating at that time and Marlene should return the next day, however he also said he didn't think it was broken and Marlene was to walk on it as much as possible.

Next day Marlene accompanied by Miss Howkins limped to the hospital; it took some time as her foot was very painful. Another Dr. saw Marlene and after sending her for an x-ray asked to speak to Miss Howkins. Although Marlene didn't hear what was said, Miss Howkins turned quite red and a nurse eventually bustled in, asking Marlene if she would like a plaster cast on her foot. The ankle was broken! Next day saw Marlene in a wheelchair being pushed by Dilly. By the end of the day, Marlene knew the frustration of not being able to walk where she wanted to walk, stop where she wanted to, and also had to travel at Dilly's speed which Marlene felt was very slow. Dilly looked in all the dress shops on the way and when Marlene asked Dilly why, she said her mother had taught her "that it was so important to keep abreast of fashion". As Dilly, like all the Home girls, had never been to a shop to buy clothes and certainly wasn't about to in the foreseeable future, it was all rather a nonsense, but Marlene said nothing as if Dilly's mother crept into any conversation with Dilly, you tried to change the subject very quickly indeed. The next day saw Marlene managing on crutches, but she managed to break her cast three times and had to go to the hospital to have it renewed. Each time the nurses said they had never seen any cast with so many signatures on it and added she must have an enormous amount of friends; Marlene knew this wasn't so, but was surprised so many people, even those she had never spoken to, wanted to sign it.

When at last the cast was removed, Marlene thought about the three days she'd had to rely on Dilly to push her as each time she'd had a new cast fitted, she could not walk for a day or two, and realised that though she had been ungracious when Dilly was lecturing her on her lack of interest in fashion, Dilly had never grumbled once.

Chapter 24: Another New Start and Learning to "Fly"

It was the long summer holiday and the Home was less than half full as the girls who had Mums or Dads were on holiday with them. Watching Sister Helena-Mary knitting one morning while she supervised breakfast gave Marlene an idea, so after breakfast, chapel, toilet and jobs, Marlene sought out Sister Helena-Mary. She listened to Marlene's request and told her to come back after lunch. The hours sped by as Marlene read "Little Lord Fauntleroy" for the second or third time.

After the Sisters' lunch Marlene presented herself once more at St. Peter's door (this was the Sisters' sitting room). For the first and probably the last time, unless she was making the fire, Sister Helena-Mary invited Marlene into the hallowed room. On the table were various balls of wool, needles and a sheet of paper covered in what looked like hieroglyphics. Sister Helena-Mary explained it was a pattern that you followed in order to make the item you were knitting. She showed Marlene the rudiments of the two stitches she would need; Marlene had decided to make mittens for Dawn for winter; she hoped the mittens would keep Dawn's hands warm so the chilblains wouldn't hurt so much. Sister Helena-Mary then explained the hieroglyphics, which were really only abbreviations for the stitches and such like. She told Marlene to have a go on her own and come back after tea and chapel, but before the Sisters' supper.

After the short lesson, Marlene crept up to her bedroom so she could work in peace and by teatime had already done several inches. At the right time Marlene once again made her way to St Peter's room, but this time Sister Helena-Mary just had a quick look and then counted the stitches. Marlene asked her why she'd counted them and she explained that if the number had been wrong, then Marlene had either increased or decreased by mistake, but everything was ok. Sister Helena Mary was so pleased with her progress; she gave Marlene a different pattern, this time for a scarf and invited her to pick out some wool. By the end of the week, Marlene had finished the scarf and, even though she could now read the instructions and knit, she was becoming bored with the plain stitching and asked Sister Helena Mary if she could try something else. Again Sister Helena Mary gave her another pattern, this time a small child's jumper; she carefully went over the pattern with Marlene, explaining how to decrease and increase stitches and then told her to come back if she forgot how to do it or had problems.

A fortnight later Marlene returned to Sister Helena Mary with the finished jumper. Sister Helena Mary was very surprised and wanted to know how she'd managed to put it together; Marlene explained that Miss Darnell had shown her how to do it, but as a precaution Marlene had sat in the sewing room while she did it. Marlene also proudly displayed two blood-stained fingers where she had pricked herself. Sister Helena-Mary said it was good enough to put in the annual Sale of Work that the "great and the good" organised in order to get extra funds for the Home. At last, after only a month, Sister Helena Mary deemed it time for Marlene to make a sweater for herself and arranged for both of them to go to town to choose the wool and pattern. Thus Marlene got started on the hobby which would last as long as her fingers were able. Sister Helena-Mary told her that at the Home's annual Sale of Work her child's jumper could have been sold several times over; Marlene was pleased as she had listened for a whole year to Dawn extolling her own smocked aprons that she had put into the Sale of work and now had something of her own to boast about.

Marlene had been thinking about how long it took to run down all the stairs now she was on the top floor. Lately she had been swinging really high on the swing and launching herself into space, carefully marking where she landed so she could "fly" further the next time. She wondered if she could somehow jump several stairs at a time and thus save time so she could read and knit longer. At first Marlene only jumped two steps, then four, then six. She was sure then that she should be able to jump the whole staircase, some thirteen steps. She could do six which was half way, so Marlene reasoned, if she launched herself off the top step, then used both arms to push against the side of the wall and the banister, to give her extra impetus in the middle it would be no more difficult than jumping the six which, with a little practice, had almost become second nature to her. Marlene carefully looked all round to make sure she was alone then tried it: to her surprise it worked so well she was nearly at the next staircase. This, then became her usual mode of travelling, even though she was still very careful only to jump when she was sure there was no-one about.

The dog days of August drifted past and soon it was time for school again. All the girls who had been away with their various parents were back to face the humdrum routine of the daily tasks. Marlene was to go to the "big" school, the Harpur Central School, by St. Paul's Church. Rosie, her co-conspirator in the "Cockroach" saga, was also going to the Harpur school, for the first time. They wore thick grey long socks and Rosie told her she hated them and would buy some white ankle socks; Marlene didn't believe her as they had no money apart from their pocket money which only amounted to a penny or two, if they were lucky, which Marlene never was! There were always too many ways your pocket money was deducted, such as not eating your dinner, being in the "Sisters' garden, not doing your daily jobs properly or being late for anything, and Marlene lost so much money, she was invariably in Sister Maud's debt! Dawn who had been placed in the "A" class when she first went to the Harpur school, couldn't understand why Marlene was in the "B" class, but Marlene didn't enlighten her!

She soon settled down and found she could do the work very easily, so to stop herself from being bored, she went to the Public Library after school and asked if she could borrow some books. The librarian gave her a form, but when Marlene said she was from St. Etheldreda's Home, the librarian smiled and gave her a card. Marlene explained that she didn't have anywhere to keep a card, so the librarian smiled again and put it in a drawer near the counter, telling Marlene to tell the duty librarian where it was. Marlene now had a problem: she wasn't sure how Sister Maud would react to her joining the library without permission and so she couldn't take out lots of books in case she got caught. Then she had a brainwave: she could keep just a couple of books in her desk at school and only take one of them home at night. Hugely satisfied that she would now have lots to do at school, she felt that this period was set to become the happiest stage of her short life. As soon as Marlene arrived at school in the morning and after the Assembly, which the whole school attended, she scampered back to her classroom armed with books and knitting; Marlene felt she was in Paradise. During lessons she put away her knitting, but there was always an open book on her lap, and after several of her teachers tried to trip her up by asking her questions on the current work, they soon grew fed up as she was also able to keep half an ear on what was going on in the classroom.

Marlene dashed down to Miss Darnell as soon as she arrived back from school to share her news and ask a very big favour. She had been chosen to take part in the school play of "Hansel and Gretel" and she was to be Gretel!! She wanted a green skirt, white blouse, a laced black waistcoat and white socks. Every rehearsal was wonderful and Marlene had never felt so excited about anything. On the stage she wouldn't be a "dirty smelly Home-kid": she would be Gretel with her beautiful white blouse and her velvet black laced waistcoat. When Miss Darnell finally produced her costume, she tried it on and went straight to Miss Howkins to have her shoulder length blond hair brushed. She was absolutely "over the moon" and then some. She showed everyone her dance, even Maggie and Maggie's cats. Marlene finally took the costume Miss Darnell had made her into school and showed Miss Newbold, who was putting on the play. Marlene asked her if she would like her to try her costume on and do the three dances she's been practicing. Miss Newbold looked at her in a very strange way and said that perhaps another time would be better as she had to go and see the Headmaster. Marlene immediately offered to go with her and show the Head her costume and the dances, but Miss Newbold just looked at her again and said that it wouldn't be necessary.

The next day Miss Newbold sent for Marlene and told her that the Headmaster had decided that only the "A" class should be allowed to be in the play, so Marlene and her costume would not be needed. Marlene was devastated! She knew her own lines and dances as well as everyone else's, and found it very hard to accept that the play was finished as far as she was concerned. After this Marlene became even more withdrawn; it seemed to her that she would never be anything except a "dirty smelly Home kid"!

Chapter 25: Introduction to a New Sport

It was September and Marlene had been at her new school for a week; she was in the same class as Rosie, the "B" class. All her class had been told to bring their swimming things the next day, so Marlene had gone to see Miss Darnell when she got home from school to ask if she had any "swimming things". Miss Darnell told her they would be on her bed by the morning and so they were. The "things" were a funny shade of pink and were very heavy; it consisted of a one piece knitted garment that came down almost to her knees and a white rubber cap which pulled at her scalp and was very uncomfortable. Directly after the register had been taken, her class had been marched down to the swimming baths which were only a short walk past the police station and over the cattle market. They all lined up and the boys were shown to their changing rooms before the girls were directed to the other side of the pool for theirs. Rosie was nowhere to be seen, but as teachers had noticed that Marlene and Rosie seldom talked, no one ever bothered to ask her where Rosie was.

It was a warm September day, almost an "Indian Summer" and, after the girls had changed, they all lined up outside the boys' changing rooms. Marlene noticed that there was a wide discrepancy in costumes. Many of the girls were in neat colourful costumes, but poor Sheila, who usually wore a jumper with holes in it so you could see her nipples, wore an even bigger costume than Marlene. She'd noticed that Sheila wore the jumper every day and she always looked very cold. Marlene had never really thought about who wore what or which child came to school with smart clothes. She knew that before every assembly Mr Mendip called out a boy called Blake and, shouting at him so loudly that the whole school knew what was happening; he took him to the cloakroom for a wash. Blake, who was quite small, always looked pinched and cold like Sheila. Marlene also noticed that most of the children in the "A" and "B" classes usually dressed quite smartly and wondered why that was.

Mr "Jack" Williams, as opposed to Mr. "Judge" Williams, asked the children who could swim. Marlene knew that the so-called swimming she had done in Maryport wasn't the real thing, as although she and Dawn had lain down like star fish and the tide had gently carried them forward, they hadn't moved their bodies at all; she kept quiet. Only a few hands went up. All boys!! Marlene thought quickly. How hard could it be if boys could do it? She came to a decision and slowly raised her hand. Everyone looked astonished: children learnt to swim in the river and the whole school knew that "Home kids" weren't allowed out except in a "crocodile" and then only to the Golf Club at Biddenham or up Manton Lane and down past the Modern School baths, or sometimes along the Clapham road, so Marlene couldn't possibly have learnt to swim. Mr Williams looked hard at her. Marlene said nothing so Mr Williams called her bluff. First he told all the girls and the boys who couldn't swim to get in the shallow part of the pool, which was separated from the deep end by a wire fence. There was also a wire fence around the whole swimming baths, which was supposed to keep the water rats out, but as the fence had been nibbled and there were holes in it, that strategy didn't really work. The baths were just part of the river something which Marlene was to learn to her cost in the future. Mr Williams pointed to the steps in the deeper part and told Marlene to get in and swim. She was caught out. Truth to tell she had never seen anyone swimming and she didn't have a clue how to do it. She was going to be found out in a lie and very publicly too!

The boys who could swim were getting restless, which gave Marlene an idea. Trying to look as shy as she could, she suggested to Mr Williams that the boys go first. It worked! Mr Williams ordered the boys in and Marlene watched them closely as they swam; she saw that most of the boys seemed to swim by just doing a bicycle movement with their arms and kicking their legs. Marlene entered the water without being asked. She shut her eyes, waved her arms about like she had seen the boys do and, to her amazement and relief, she travelled four or five yards through the water. She'd proved them all wrong, even herself. She really could swim!!

Marlene spent the rest of the lesson, virtually on her own, using dogged determination first to do five strokes, if one could call her uncoordinated splashing strokes, and then eight, then ten. Towards the end of the lesson a man came over to talk to her. He was the swimming superintendent, Mr Jack Nash and he'd been watching her closely. He had quickly deduced that she had never swum before this lesson. He asked her how she had been so sure she could swim, and she told him that she hadn't, but she'd thought if boys could swim, girls could too. He laughed at this and then told her about the certification system at the baths and that next week she should try to swim 10 yards and get her first certificate. Mr Nash also mentioned that the swimming baths was open Saturday afternoons, at least for the next two weeks.

When Marlene got out of the pool, if that was what the fenced-off part of the river next door to the gasworks could be called, the weight of the knitted costume had dragged it down so it was almost as low as Sheila's. Marlene couldn't wait to get home at lunchtime to tell Sister Helena-Mary about her exploits. She usually told her about things, rather than Sister Maud, as she was, like all the girls, slightly in awe of Sister Maud, as she was the one who chastised the girls, whether they warranted it or not.

Marlene still didn't enjoy lunch, possibly because of the eight years she'd spent dreading it and, as she had only been able to eat a sliver of meat at a time, mealtimes had been agonisingly slow. Sister Helena-Mary was luckily on duty so after dinner she told her about the certificates and that Mr Nash had said she should be able to swim the 10 yards next week. Sister Helena-Mary surprisingly gave her permission straight away but, not wanting to "push her luck", Marlene didn't tell her about Saturday afternoons as she had decided she didn't need to "climb that mountain" 'till next year, particularly as the swimming baths were only going to be open two more weeks.

The next week, she and six of the boys were asked to get out of the water and led to some steps in a different part of the pool. Mr Nash had already talked to her, telling her that she could swim the distance easily, so she got straight in the water while the boys waited on the side. Mr Williams was helping the non-swimmers, so Mr Nash pointed out the distance and, holding a big pole in front of her, he walked beside her while she swam. She went under twice, coughing loudly, but Mr Nash had been so sure she could do it, she couldn't contemplate giving up. When she reached the marker she heard Mr Williams' Welsh accent shouting congratulations and Mr Nash's whisper of well done. Marlene had done it! The first person in her class to get a certificate! Four boys also swam the distance, but the other two had to try the next time. Mr Nash told her at the end of the lesson it would be sixpence for the certificate, but when he saw the sadness in her eyes and when she told him she was from St. Etheldreda's Home and didn't have money, he pretended he'd got a spare one.

Marlene had noticed that only girls from the "A" class were in the school netball team. This offended her sense of fairness and she decided she **would** be in the school team. She thought long and hard about how she would manage this. Marlene knew that nothing would change just by asking; the only way into the team was by making herself indispensible. The only person in a netball team that could really stand out was the shooter so every break she asked Miss Flitwick, who took them for netball, for a ball and practised shooting.. It wasn't long before she could demonstrate to Miss Flitwick that she was a player who had to be taken seriously.

Chapter 26: The Variety of Routine

Marlene raked the board with her eyes; the new rotas were up and she needed to know what her morning job was. They only had half an hour to do it so if you had a difficult one, you were pushed for time. The worst one was making the Sisters' fire in St Peter's. All the rooms were named after saints rather than numbers or conventional names such as a sitting room or dining room as there were at least five sitting rooms. St Peters was the nuns' sitting room and if you made a mess, which Marlene invariably did, then it had to be cleared up before you had breakfast .It meant you had to hurry with dressing and washing and making your bed so you could squeeze a few minutes more from the carefully worked schedule. With relief, she saw she was down to clean the Sisters' landing and both sets of stairs. It was a very large area that came under the close scrutiny of Sister Maud, but it was doable.

The week-day job was to sweep and dust, and then on Saturday she would have the additional task of polishing both sets of stairs and the huge landing, which ran from the front of the house to the back; it wasn't as bad as fire-lighting as she was in control. The problem with lighting fires was there were too many variables: the sticks and coal could be damp or the matches might be difficult to strike, even the wind could be in the wrong direction! All these prevented you from doing the job easily and quickly. Fortunately, none of these applied to just general cleaning; a broom and a dust-pan and brush would suffice in the week and at the weekend, well sometimes it was fun, as you could tie dusters over your socks once you had put the polish on and then just "skate" on the floor to shine it. Often she could persuade others to join in the fun so the floor would be done in no time and even Sister Maud, when she inspected, could find nothing to complain about. The stairs were a different matter, though; with two flights of thirteen stairs, they would take the most time. The stairs from the children's bedrooms to the Sisters' landing were not too bad as they were mostly in darkness, but the stairs leading down to the Sisters' hall had three sets of windows and there were always nuns and staff going backwards and forwards, so these had to be done properly.

She looked down the list a little further and saw Dawn's name opposite fire lighting in St. Peter's. Poor Dawn!! Her chilblains had already started, for it was November, and although they weren't too bad at the moment, Dawn would suffer as the hard coals and sticks and even just scrunching up the paper would break open the scabs from the chilblains and cause her more pain. Dawn's hands were a little better outside due to Marlene's hand knitted mittens, but she couldn't wear them when she cleaned the grate and lit the fires. Marlene then looked at the next list of duties which allocated washing up, laying and clearing the tables, cleaning the refectory floor and peeling the next day's potatoes; with thirty girls in the Home, plus another ten staff potato peeling could be a very time consuming job; even scanning the lists took time. Marlene spotted her name with Dilly's and saw they would be laying the tea tables and, because there were two of them, they would also have to sweep the floor after tea. This was one of the better duties as, unlike breakfast and lunch time which were always rushed as they had to get back to school on time, they could take their time. She also liked working with Dilly as although you had to take charge, she was a good worker as long as you told her repeatedly what, when, where and how to do anything.

In November there were extra jobs such as peeling apples and bottling and preparing fruit and vegetables which had been donated by "the great and good". One Saturday morning in early October as fifteen or so of the older girls were peeling apples round the big kitchen table, Marlene made up what was to become "their" anthem. She and the girls sang it to the tune of the missionary hymn: "There is a Happy Land" and it was always sung with great gusto, much to Sister Maud's annoyance.

There is an unhappy home in Bedfordshire,
Where we get grumbled at all through the year.

Grumble, grumble all the day, never get a bit of pay,
That's why we gradually fade, fade away

It became almost a necessity to sing it whenever several of the girls were engaged in some chore together

In the summer they sometimes visited the enormous (even by the Home's standards) mansions, which were the abodes of "the great and the good", where they would pick currants, strawberries, raspberries and gooseberries. It usually took a whole afternoon. You didn't actually ever see" the great and the good", only the gardeners, but although the fruit picked was collected by the housekeeper, at least half was consumed by the girls!! There was sometimes an opportunity to paddle in the ponds and rivers on the estates which was great fun. The girls used their commodious knickers to prevent their skirts getting wet. Marlene remembered, with a smile, going to the Lord Lieutenant of the County, Simon Whitbread's, estate and Pru, who was quite fat anyway, getting her big thighs caught in a cattle grid. They all pulled and pushed, accompanied by Pru's woeful screams and cries. Eventually grown-ups were alerted and came running and, after much examining of Pru's leg and even more manoeuvring, which made the poor girl's shrieks even louder, one of the staff had a brainwave and went to get some butter, which she slapped on the trapped leg and a very woebegone Pru was finally free. Still, Marlene thought, it had brightened up the afternoon; indeed it had been quite an adventure.

However, for the next few weeks she really was in clover as far as jobs went, as the ones allocated to her were "easy-peasy". Marlene didn't ever think that it was really putting off the inevitable and that next time she might well have one of the less easy jobs to do. If she had really thought about it she would have realised that to do the Sisters' fires in the dead of winter, having to collect the chopped kindling and the coal from outside, would be considerably worse than doing it in late autumn, when just a broom and duster were all that were needed!

Chapter 27: White Socks and into the "Pit!"

Winter was here and Dawn's hands were bloody; if anything, she had more chilblains than ever before as they'd had a cold November and she was crying with pain most mornings. One December morning, Marlene found herself walking to school with Rosie, something she rarely did as usually she walked on her own or with Dilly. Once they had passed through the gate, Rosie asked her to wait a minute. Then, to her surprise, Rosie took off her shoes, peeled off her long grey socks and from her pocket drew a white pair of ankle socks. Marlene stared in amazement as Rosie put them on, laced up her shoes and put her grey socks in her pocket; Marlene asked her where she'd got them and Rosie muttered something about her mother. Marlene couldn't remember Rosie having a mother but, as she really hadn't taken much notice of what Rosie did or what visitors she had, she said nothing. When they got to school, they both went their separate ways as they rarely spoke to each other in school, even though they were in the same class. There was no animosity between them, but there was no real friendship either as they didn't have anything in common.

Thursday evenings were Guide night; the Guides met in St. Martin's church hall on the same night and at the same time as the Sea Cadets met in their old infant and junior school, Clapham Road, which was next door. They had a bugler in their outfit and the sound of the bugle would accompany their walk to Guides. Once inside the Hall, if you listened carefully, you could just hear the faint and somewhat eerie strains of "Taps" in the air. They sang Taps at the close of Guides:

> *Day is gone, from the sun,*
> *From the hills, from the sky.*
> *All is well. Safely rest. God is nigh*

161

but hearing the sound of the bugle sweet and clear and then fading away on the last note somehow made the night time darker, more real.

Marlene liked Guides, maybe because she was very quick at passing the various badges, maybe because the meetings were ordered and at Guides there were no "dirty smelly Home kids", just Guides, or may be because it was a break from the monotony of the "daily round, the common task". To be truthful she didn't really know, but she did know she looked forward to the meetings. Easter came and they were told they were going to camp. Marlene wasn't sure what "camp" was, but everyone seemed very excited by it. Dawn, Dilly, Elsie and several other Home girls were going also so an early April morning saw them carrying huge bags to St. Martin's church hall. School had finished for Easter, so Marlene supposed this was a kind of holiday. She had been made a lieutenant, and had a white lanyard and a whistle, both of which she was very proud of. She had looked up "camp" in a dictionary, but apart from reading that it was a group of tents, as used by the army, the information was pretty sketchy.

After a long bus ride they arrived in a FIELD!!! They all tumbled from the bus and Marlene looked round anxiously for the tents. There was nothing in the field at all except a couple of trees on the far side. Their Guide Captain called all the lieutenants together and pointing to some bundles which had been unloaded from the bus, informed them that they were their tents. Captain also pointed to some sticks in heaps on the ground and some ropes and then appointed one of the accompanying adults to each patrol, telling the Guides that these people would show them how to set up their tent. Marlene's adult was called Miss Brown and, judging from her face, she was not best pleased to be there.

Miss Brown led the group to a patch of ground and told them to put the equipment down and then pointed to the bundle of material that apparently was their tent. She then told them to lay it out flat on the ground; this proved problematical as the tent did not want to be laid flat! Miss Brown was now very "unpleased!" Marlene caught the word "idiots" as

Miss Brown mumbled and grumbled. Marlene asked her group if any of them had been camping before, but no one had. Miss Brown then seized a corner of the material and informed them through clenched teeth that the corner was the top of the tent. Next she pointed to the sticks and told them to thread them through the small holes at the bottom of the tent and then push them in the ground. Then she stalked off. Marlene glanced round the field; other groups were laughing and their adult was leading from the front, as it were. Dilly, who was in Marlene's group, had no idea at all, which was the norm, but unfortunately Marlene didn't have much idea either. She sent another guide, Betty, to look at the other groups but, since the other tents looked to be nearly up as they'd actually got the guy ropes on and were raising the tent, it wasn't much use.

A bell rang which was the signal for all lieutenants to report to the Captain. Marlene went over. It was now past lunchtime and the captain told them that when their tent was up, they could send someone to the cook's tent to get some sandwiches, after which most of them could spend the time unpacking their things and then could relax. As she said "most of them" she glanced meaningfully at Marlene and said that the patrol that was last would also have to dig the latrines. Marlene had no idea what latrines were, but from the Captain's expression, it was not a choice activity! Marlene looked around once more and saw that all the tents were well on the way to being put up except one - hers. She looked for Miss Brown, but couldn't see her so she plucked up courage and approached the Captain. Marlene told the Captain of their dilemma: none of them had ever pitched a tent before and Miss Brown could not be found. The Captain looked at her for a long time before telling her that they had been so rude to Miss Brown that she had left the camp and probably was not coming back, therefore her team was on its own. Marlene remonstrated with the Captain, but to no avail. Her team spent the next three hours trying to pitch the tent. They had no sandwiches and the girls were all either grumbling or crying. In the end Marlene let one of them go and fetch some food, hoping the Captain wouldn't spot them.

The tent was at last looking a little like the real thing and Marlene was just about to go and find out about the latrines when the bell rang once more. This time the Captain told them that each team had to light a cooking fire and once that was done, they could go to the cooks' tent to get the food they were to cook. She also told Marlene that, as Miss Brown had indeed left the site, it was most unlikely she would be returning; they really were on their own!

Marlene had delegated four girls out of the six in her patrol to go and get instructions on how and where to dig the latrines and she and Dilly got on with the fire. She had lit several fires, as that was one of the chores in the Home, so she knew the basics. Perhaps this was something she could do more easily than most. Marlene sent Dilly off to get sticks and kindling while she dug a small pit. Dilly soon got back with the sticks and kindling and within minutes the fire was blazing well.

Marlene debated as to whether she could trust Dilly to go to the cook's tent to get food, but decided against it and asked her to watch the fire while she went for the food. The food was all laid out with their patrol names on so she took the one marked "Robin" and went back to her fire. As she was returning, she called to Dilly to go and check how the others were doing. Marlene lit the fire and, hearing a noise behind her, turned round and saw Dilly absolutely filthy and crying. Stifling a sigh she asked Dilly what had happened. Dilly said the latrines were a huge ditch, very narrow, that you had to go to the toilet in, and the rest of the patrol had pushed her in. Marlene dried Dilly's tears, sent her into the tent to change and then rounded up her errant patrol. Marlene felt she had to get the patrol on-side, as it were, but as she was younger than some of them and there had already been murmurings of favouritism it would be difficult. She led them up the field out of earshot of the rest of the camp and told them of her predicament. Marlene explained that Dilly was defenceless and that what they had done was very cruel. She explained that they were already in the Captain's bad books because of Miss Brown and if she had to report this incident to the Captain, all the patrol might well be sent home. She asked them to think about it and went to check on Dilly, who, she found, had now almost forgotten the incident. Marlene showed her how to feed the fire and went back to her patrols, who were now looking decidedly sorry for themselves.

She asked them if they had any thoughts on what should be done and was relieved when her friend Janet, asked whether they could avoid telling the Captain about the latrine incident and then make a real effort to be the best patrol, even without Miss Brown! Marlene was delighted, but frowned and pretended she had to consider this very carefully. Of course, in the end she agreed, but only as long as, in recompense, they allowed Dilly as much food as she liked, just for that one evening, and that they also cleared the fire when they'd cooked and washed up. They readily agreed and peace was restored. Dilly couldn't understand why everyone was so nice to her and the Captain came over and congratulated them on how quickly the fire and cooking had been done and how clean their little bit of the campsite was. Marlene and the Robin patrol went to bed happy.

The week passed quickly as Marlene began to relax and enjoy this departure from the usual routine. Her patrol also became more adept and soon they were easily the best patrol. The Captain must have agreed with her, as when she announced the results of the daily competition, the Robin Patrol invariably came out on top. However, it is amazing how, just when you think nothing can ever go wrong, fate is just waiting for the right moment to trip you up!

It was Friday morning, the penultimate day of camp and it had been raining; in fact it had been raining so much that they had had to cook all their supper on Thursday evening on a big communal fire which the Captain and some of the other adults made, as it was too wet to light individual fires. Some of the girls had been caught out, as although the Captain had warned them repeatedly not to leave belongings outside the tent, some of them hadn't checked that everything was inside and of course clothes, particularly nightclothes had got very wet. Marlene, by a stroke of genius, had appointed Dilly as the person who checked two or three times daily that everything was within the confines of the tent and although most of them got very irritated by Dilly's continual nagging, they soon realised the only way to shut her up was to move their things. Marlene thought about this; yes, Dilly hadn't "two brain cells to rub together", but she certainly had her uses and in some situations she really was the "best man for the job!" It meant none of her patrol had wet clothes, an enormous relief. When the Captain praised the Robin Patrol again, Marlene was quick to point out that it was Dilly who had ensured that all their things were kept dry.

The next morning, after dressing, Marlene had to visit the latrines. All the Guides had got used to straddling the ditch when going to the toilet and now, after nearly a week, thought nothing of it. The Robin Patrol had had the unpleasant task of filling in the ditch along with two other patrols, as the captain insisted it was done every other day. One patrol filled in the ditch whilst another patrol dug the new one, but as filling in didn't take as long as digging, they hadn't grumbled too much. In fact, it was yet another good story to tell their families, maybe with a little embellishment, but surely that was the whole point of doing something out of the ordinary. Anyway Marlene gaily made her way to the latrines, humming and without a care in the world; they had nearly got to the end of the week and, although she was the youngest lieutenant, her patrol had done very well. The ground was very wet and muddy, but Marlene gave little thought as to the consequences of the rain. She was in full uniform, her whistle brightly polished and her lanyard showing up a pristine white against the royal blue of her uniform. They had all put on full uniform, instead of shorts and t-shirts, as they were going on a trip on the coach later.

Marlene straddled the latrine and was nearly finished when disaster struck! Her feet slipped on the greasy mud and she fell right into the latrine!! She scrambled out with great difficulty, looking all round to see if anyone had seen her, but no one was about. She looked down at her pristine lanyard, now a dull brown colour, and the rest of her uniform now covered with the whole camp's excrement. She had no idea what to do. She was too ashamed just to go back and laugh it off. Then she suddenly realised that her bright silver whistle was missing. Her heart stopped as she realised she had two choices: she could leave it where it undoubtedly was and try to explain to Sister Maud that she'd lost it, or do the unthinkable! If Marlene left it where it was, she knew the whistle wouldn't be replaced and so very reluctantly and pinching her nose to try to stop some of the dreadful smell, she jumped into the latrine gagging all the time. She felt in the muck with one hand whilst still pinching her nose with the other. She soon realised the terrible job would be done quicker if she used both hands and so she eventually found the whistle. One problem solved, but there seemed an even higher mountain to climb. How was she to get back into camp without everyone finding out and laughing at her? "Dilly!" she thought. Another good thing about Dilly was she had little or no sense of humour, so she seldom laughed at any situation and never teased anyone or was unkind. It may well have been that she was unable to see things from an abstract point of view but, for whatever reason, Marlene was grateful. Funny, she thought, this was the second occasion Dilly had saved the day; well, almost, as she still had to put her plan into action.

Marlene crept back to her tent, first of all making sure Dilly was on her own; she was as it was rare for the girls to include her in their games, particularly if they were not from the Home. Dilly looked at her, horrified at her disgusting appearance and worse the terrible smell. Marlene quickly stripped off her uniform and dressed in her camp things. She sent Dilly to get some water and then set to, trying to get her uniform as clean as she could in the cold water and the soap they used for washing, which was all she had to hand. She knew it would not be pristine, but if it just lost the smell and the excrement then she could put stage two of her plan into action. Marlene rinsed her uniform thoroughly; poor Dilly had to make several trips to where the fresh water was stored, until at last Marlene was satisfied and, after thanking Dilly from the bottom of her heart, made her way to the Captain. Holding up her wet uniform, she explained that she had carelessly slipped on the mud, knocking over a bucket of water. The Captain, who had begun to think of Marlene as a very competent Guide, told her to rig up a washing line near the cooks' tent and wear her camp clothes until her uniform was dry.

Things had gone according to plan, but Marlene realised that without Dilly's co-operation she would have been ridiculed. This in turn made her acknowledge that, although a quick brain was very useful, someone with Dilly's nature could be invaluable and that, perhaps, everyone had his or her uses. Marlene thought about the miserable Miss Brown and realised that, because of her, the team had been forced to learn to co-operate and had "gelled" far more quickly than the other teams and had thus become a far more competent and more cohesive team. So even people like Miss Brown had their uses! The next day they all returned home with adventures to relate, but Marlene never forgot the lessons she had learned and never told anyone of them.

Guide Camp 1954

Elsie on far right

Chapter 28: Steeple Jacks and Barred Windows.

Marlene was wandering through the dormitories on the third floor; she was going to fetch a book she'd hidden under her pillow. She was lost in thought as usual when she heard Dawn whispering to her, calling her name. Marlene looked all round, but couldn't see her sister. "Over here," Dawn said in a voice still hushed but a bit louder. Marlene looked up and down the "through" dormitory, which was really two rooms with the middle door removed to make more space and allow the staff to see both rooms more easily. Marlene still couldn't see anybody, but now Moira called her and then she saw them: Dawn, Moira and Ethel, all standing on a little platform outside the dormer window. "Come out, Marlene!" Dawn insisted. Marlene didn't really want to, as she'd got to an interesting part of "A Tale of Two Cities." It was one of the few Dickens stories she liked as he didn't address the reader directly so much. She hated it when he broke off the story with "And now my dear reader…." She was quite capable of following the story and disliked the intrusion of the writer. When Marlene read a book, she wanted to travel through time and space and Dickens's many interruptions meant that she was reminded constantly that it was only a book and that she wasn't travelling anywhere! She also liked "A Tale of Two Cities", as, according to Miss Newbold, she was playing a prominent part in the book, namely Madam Defarge!!Apparently Madam Defage would sit and watch the aristocrats being guillotined whilst knitting continuously.

However, Moira was there and unless she really wanted to prove a point or it was a matter of principle, she usually humoured Moira, so out she stepped through the window. She asked Dawn what they were doing. Dawn told her they were going to climb the roof. When Marlene asked the obvious question, Dawn couldn't say why they were doing it and when Marlene asked the next very obvious question, Dawn had forgotten whose idea it was. Marlene looked at the roof; it looked very steep and slippery as it had rained the night before. Marlene thought of many good reasons why she shouldn't climb it, but settled in the end for going last. She reasoned there was little room on the roof, so perhaps when the other three had got to the top, they would then come down and Marlene might not actually have to go up She wasn't afraid of heights, but could see little point in it, and she did want to find out what was going to happen to Sidney when he arrived in Paris at the height of the French Revolution. So she fixed what she hoped was a look of "derring-do" on her face and followed them up the roof, albeit at a distance. The roof was very high, as the building comprised three high-ceilinged floors whose height was increased by large attics .Marlene looked down and paled at the view: it was a very long way down!

Suddenly Marlene heard a very strange and strangled scream. She was almost at the pinnacle and, peering over, she saw Maggie. They'd never heard Maggie scream before and it heralded a mass exodus as they slipped and slid down the steep pitch of the roof. But they weren't fast enough, as when they'd climbed through the window and started down the stairs, they were met by Miss Howkins, who rounded them up and took them to The Office, where a very cross looking Sister Maude was waiting. She didn't whip them, but told them she had already sent for someone to fix bars on all the third floor windows and that they would all pay seven shillings and sixpence out of their pocket money. Marlene thought that was a very weak punishment especially as she never got any pocket money anyway. She still owed a fortune from the time she had wet the bed and when she couldn't eat her food so would probably still be paying it when she finally left the home and anyway, Sidney was waiting.

The bars were put up and life returned to normal. Sidney had been executed and it was *"a far, far better thing....."* and now Marlene was reading Baroness Orczy's account of Sir Percy Blakeney's exploits in Paris at the same time. Peace was restored, at least for the time being!

Chapter 29: At Last...A Mystery Solved? Well Almost!

Netball had finished with the spring term, but in the last week of the netball season Miss Flitwick had sent for Marlene and told her that because she had been practising shooting every day, she was now the best shooter Miss Flitwick had ever seen, and in the Autumn term she was to play for the school team. Marlene was so pleased she was lost for words; to get into the team had been her plan, but she had never been really sure it would work! Now the season had finished, everyone had to walk or cycle to the school field, which was nearer Clapham than Bedford, or so Marlene thought, but with the promise of a place in the school team, Marlene still practised her shooting every break-time.

One day, as it was raining and Miss Flitwick was away from school. Marlene mooched round the playground. At first she put the book she was reading under her coat, making sure it didn't get wet, but she got so fed up as she found it impossible to read as people kept pushing her, so she decided to go to her next lesson early. It was Geography with Mr "Jack" Williams.

The two Mr. Williams could hardly have been more different. "Judge" Williams was quite tall and very round; he loved to tell stories so they seldom did much class work. Even when the class was actually working, it was easy to side-track him by asking an innocent sounding question that was vaguely, usually very vaguely, connected to the work, just to start him off. As he taught Religious Instruction and probably Marlene knew as much about the Bible as he did, it usually fell to Marlene to ask the question, especially as it was in her own interest, as she could then lose herself in a book for the rest of the lesson.

Mr "Jack" Williams was totally different; he was quite small and thin, but with that wiry strength you often find in small thin people. He was very Welsh and was an inspired music teacher and choirmaster He was very strict, but fair,however, he was always very nice to her; she might even have described him as avuncular if she'd ever had an uncle to compare him with.

She climbed the fire escape stairs to his classroom and after looking all round, she quietly opened the door and stared in surprise: Rosie was spread-eagled across two or three desks, surrounded by boys. Marlene couldn't actually see what was happening and by now everyone in the room had frozen into a quite bizarre tableau. Marlene called out to Rosie to see if she needed help, but Rosie shouted at her to go away and leave her alone as she was "busy". To say Marlene was perplexed would have been a huge understatement, as she couldn't understand how Rosie could be busy just lying on the desk! Marlene quickly retreated and propped herself against the wall of the corridor and went back to reading her book. If she had been more street-wise, she would have been able to solve the problem of how Rosie got her white socks, but she wasn't, so she couldn't. Eventually Mr "Jack" Williams and the rest of the class clattered up the iron steps and the lesson began. His lessons were usually quite interesting and she instinctively knew that reading her book was not an option so the lesson trundled on.

On the way home to dinner, Marlene thought about the episode with Rosie. She wanted to ask Rosie about it, but wasn't sure what to ask; it wasn't 'till some years after she'd left school that she managed to solve the mystery. Rosie had started to get quite fat and her brassiere looked to be far too small. Marlene kept thinking she should tell Rosie to see Miss Howkins and ask for a bigger one, but she was too bound up with her various activitieknitting and reading.. Rosie was sent away from the Home eighteen months later, but her sister Penny stayed at the Home. Although it was quite common practice for girls to come and go without explanation, they never left without their sisters and, eventually, some years later, Marlene put two and two together and guessed what had happened.

All the girls in her class were now cooking, with the exception of Marlene, who still hadn't finished her apron; all the girls were required to make an apron to wear in

Domestic Science before they were allowed to cook. One or two of them had finished theirs in a month, most in three months and the rest in five months, but Marlene still hadn't finished; her punishment was that she had to sit on her own in the sewing room until she finished it. Marlene was delighted, as because she was on her own, out came her knitting and the current book and Marlene was in heaven. Eventually, Miss Flitwick threw her despised apron at her and told her to take it home and bring it back finished in a week. Marlene thought about telling her that, because she was in the Home, she couldn't do that. Then she thought of Miss Darnell and the problem was solved, much to Marlene's satisfaction, even though she would miss the peaceful hour she'd spent every week doing the things she wanted to do.

As it was the summer term, the swimming baths had opened and Marlene was one of their most dedicated and loyal customers. She went every Saturday afternoon, rain or shine, and in the first month had been awarded her prized certificates for fifty, seventy-five and a hundred yards. Each time Jack had told her he had lots of spare certificates so she didn't have to pay.

When Marlene went swimming with the school, she was left very much to her own devices; however one day the teacher who always took them swimming, Mr Jack Williams asked her to report to him once she was changed. Marlene was quite apprehensive at first, but when she went over to him Marlene saw there were half a dozen boys there too. Mr Williams explained he was going to teach them to dive so they could get their "Elementary" certificate. Marlene was excited; swimming held no fears for her as she was now very much at home in the water. Mr Williams lined them up and the first boy dived in, making a loud splash that Mr Williams told them was a belly-flop. Marlene was third in the queue, but as she was standing on the side, the boy in front of her dived in and didn't surface! Then, to Marlene's consternation, the water turned red! Jack Nash, who was the swimming bath manager, had been alerted by the kerfuffle and immediately dived in still in his clothes. He brought the boy out, still alive but with a bleeding cut on his head. To Marlene's utter amazement, Mr Williams told Marlene it was her turn. What was she waiting for? Marlene looked at the red stain in the water and looked back at the teacher, but there was no help there so Marlene gathering her courage dived in for what was to be her first and last dive for the next fifteen years. She did, however, get her certificate, the youngest girl in her year and the only girl in the Home ever to have one! By the time she left the Home she would have her half mile and her mile certificates, but more importantly, swimming would be the route through which she would eventually achieve her life's ambition.

Chapter 30: "There are More Things in Heaven and Earth..."

There was great excitement in the Home; Sister Maude had told the girls that there would be workmen around the building for a few weeks. She sternly told everyone that there should be no communication with any of the men. She also said there was to be a grand new extension, which would mean there would be five new toilets and five new bathrooms on the first floor. There would also be a new corridor linking the nuns' part of the house with the girls' accommodation on the ground floor; this meant people could access both areas without having to climb the stairs to the second floor or use the "Tube".

The work was started, but soon stopped without explanation. When the reason came filtering through the reliable grape vine, of which Dawn was a key component, it almost caused group hysteria, which was probably why Sister Maude hadn't told them. A pile of bones had been found under the very window that Marlene had seen the ghostly figure of a nun all those years before! The next morning, Sister Helena Mary, who was on breakfast duty, told the girls that once again they would have to have their dinners at school just for that day. Marlene knew the two events – seeing the figure and finding the bones - were linked in some way. She didn't say anything, though, as she knew the news would either be disbelieved or some of the girls, particularly Moira's gang, would immediately pretend to be frightened and hysterical over something Marlene knew was not terrifying or evil, but a kind of communication between her and the figure.

Marlene was determined to find out exactly what was going to happen while they were at school. She'd just read a new author, Dennis Wheatley who had written a story about "Black Magic" and explained that in some cases like this an exorcism was needed. She decided to look the word up in the library that afternoon after school. All day at school Marlene was trying to figure out what it meant, so as soon as she left school that afternoon she went to the library and asked her favourite member of staff. The request was met with puzzled and anxious looks and she was asked why she wanted to know.

Marlene just told the librarian she'd read it somewhere and eventually she was told where to look. An exorcism, she read, was sometimes called "The Bell, Book and Candle" and was used sometimes to free a building or a place of evil spirits. Marlene knew the figure she'd seen was not evil, but she also guessed the ceremony had taken place in the Home when the girls were at school. She thought hard and then decided on a plan. When she got home she asked Sister Eleanor whether the ceremony had gone well; Sister Eleanor looked anxious, so Marlene asked whether they'd used the Bible. The nun floundered and then excused herself on the pretext of having to be elsewhere. Marlene had her answer!

Some of the big girls were soon in trouble as they didn't seem to be able to stay away from the workmen and Pru and Dora seemed to be the worst offenders. Marlene couldn't understand why even Dawn and Ethel changed their behaviour when they met men, either in the building or outside. They would fluff up their hair, which was extremely difficult for Dawn, as she just had two very thin plaits, and smile in a sickly sort of way. She also noted how Dawn took off her glasses when they were near the men and how Miss Howkins was having to soak the hair of many of the bigger girls before school because they'd been wearing rags all night in an attempt to curl their hair. All the staff breathed a sigh of relief when the building work was finished. The girls were delighted as they no longer had to walk down two corridors and two flights of stairs to visit the toilets, Another unexpected bonus was that both nuns and staff could clearly be seen now as they travelled down the corridor from the nuns' side of the house, giving the girls an early warning if they were engaged in illicit activities.

Chapter 31: A Near Drowning?

Marlene was undressing, ready to go down to the bathrooms when a very excited Dawn dashed in; she shouted that everyone should go down to the bathrooms as Miss Guy was trying to drown Rosie. Marlene and Dilly galloped down the stairs and were quickly hauled up to the top of the flimsy partition, which separated the bathroom, by the crowd of girls already there; there was very little room to spare and the partition was shaking from all the unaccustomed weight. One of the girls was trying to explain what was happening: apparently Rosie had been trying to get out of the bath and Miss Guy had pushed her back in and as, the girls could see quite clearly, the two of them were now battling it out. Eventually the noise attracted Miss Howkins, who was not on duty that evening, but was in her room just along the corridor. She cleared the bathroom area of excited spectators and proceeded to break the lock on the bathroom door. As Marlene, along with all the other girls, was banished from the scene, it was unclear what happened after that, but the next day at breakfast, Sister Helens-Mary told them all that Rosie was very ill with Rheumatic Fever and it would be several weeks before she was well again.

About a week later, Miss Howkins said Rosie had been asking for her and, although the doctor had left instructions that no visitors be allowed, Sister Helena-Mary felt it could do nothing but good for Marlene to visit every day for about half an hour. Marlene thought it strange that Rosie should ask for her as, although they were about the same age, she and Rosie were as different as could be. Rosie was a very well-developed and very street-wise girl who had come from London. She was very forward for her age and, in London, had listened to the radio every day and knew all the current popular songs. She especially liked Slim Whitman and knew most of his songs by heart, particularly "Rosemarie". Rosie was very particular about her appearance, hence the "white socks" saga. She disliked the Home and school and was always talking about running away, but the reality was she was just too lazy to be bothered. Marlene was very bookish, loved school and was always thinking up new games all the girls could play. Although physically she was quite thin, she was very strong. She was also very stubborn and determined, as the girls in the Home had found out several years previously. Marlene was also very under-developed and very innocent; having lived in the Home since she was three and having few friends meant that she was naïve, with little or no "street cred". After the first visit to Rosie, Marlene discovered why Rosie had asked to see her; apparently Rosie hated the medicine and so asked Marlene to have it instead. Marlene refused, but took it from her and poured it outside the window. She also realised to her surprise that Rosie hadn't made any real friends in the Home; she couldn't think why that was until a year later when things fell into place and the mystery was solved.

Marlene had made some friends in her class, but her closest friend was Janet Mallabar. Janet had told her they had to be friends as both their surnames were monkey names, Mallabar and Gibbons. Janet had a brother, Jimmie and a mum and dad. She was very kind to Marlene, as she lent her all the magazines she had. She had two magazines every month; one was "Movie Maker", which had lots of photos of film stars, but as Marlene had never been to the cinema, she wasn't as impressed as she might have been! The second magazine was more interesting, at least as far as Marlene was concerned; it was all about ballet and her dream was to be a dancer, even though she knew it wasn't ever going to happen, and, as she knew she would have to leave school at fifteen, it was also unlikely that she would ever achieve her main ambition, the one she'd had from the age of ten, which was to teach. It was strange that although Marlene knew dancing and teaching were out of the question and she had discounted dancing, she wasn't so sure about teaching. She knew it was practically impossible, but....

Janet's father worked in the car factory in the next town, but they lived by the junior school. Her mother had longed for Janet to pass her eleven-plus and go to the Public School, but Janet had failed. Now Janet, along with anyone who wanted to, was to be given another chance. Janet had begged Marlene to come with her, as Janet and her mum were convinced she would pass this time, but Marlene remembered the lucky escape she'd had two years earlier, when a chance conversation between Sister Helena-Mary and the Matron, overheard by Marlene when she was in hospital, had alerted her to the fact that it was certain she would go to the High School. Marlene had avoided it that time and she had no wish to go through that again.

Another of her school friends was Barbara, who was very beautiful, with blue black curly hair and intense blue, almost turquoise eyes. She had a bicycle and she let Marlene ride it very slowly on the way back from school. Marlene had learnt to ride during one of her visits to Stevenage, when Jennifer had said she could borrow her bike for ten minutes only; despite this, when they were in the garden and Auntie Mary couldn't hear them, Marlene had been able to ride the bike within five minutes and then spent the rest of her allotted time riding it round the garden. Marlene and Barbara walked together until they got to the Home and then Barbara rode the rest of the way home, as she lived nearly as far as the Golf Club. Marlene's other friends were Jill and the two boys that sat just behind her, Ewan and Terry. These two puzzled Marlene as they weren't like the rest of the boys. Before class each day, the other boys in the class, who were quite a bit bigger than they were, would grab them round the bottom and make them cry. Marlene hadn't a clue what they were doing and why only to these two boys. Another mystery to be solved a good deal later

Chapter 32: A Moral Dilemma and an Unanswerable Question

Marlene was now twelve, nearly thirteen, and their school had a new Head Master. Marlene still loved school and, even after the apron catastrophe, she quite enjoyed sewing classes, although she didn't do much sewing. They were making what Miss Waller called "Vanity" bags, which were barrel shaped with a draw string top. Marlene couldn't see where she would use one or who would ever want such a thing, but she liked putting the different coloured cotton reels together to see if they would "go". She also liked drawing fashionable dresses in different colours and different styles. Marlene experimented with colour, sometimes using toning colours, sometimes contrasting. She'd borrowed a book from the library which detailed the newest fashion trends and started to look critically at what her teachers were wearing. The sewing teacher seldom bothered Marlene, as most of the girls in her class loved needlework and usually one or another needed her attention; she was happy to help those girls who were working, rather than Marlene, who obviously was not motivated and was quite content to sit there playing with the cotton reels and drawing.

Changes were made, as the new Head, Mr Cantor, had altered the curriculum and had decided both A and B classes should do science, so her class now went to the science lab for their weekly science lessons. These proved very different from their other classes as the room had a funny smell and they were told they now had to do "experiments". There was also much more freedom in science classes, as the pupils were not expected to remain in their desks the whole lesson. Their teacher, a Mr. Albert Monger, could not control the class so there was also a lot of tomfoolery. This particular lesson they had been introduced to Bunsen burners" and were doing experiments on how heat could change both form and colour, depending on what was being heated. The teacher was the other side of the room when a terrible scream was heard: Terry was clutching his wrist and an iron rod was stuck to his hand. Marlene noticed Ewan, who was next to him, was white with fear. And she realised what had happened.

Mr Monger immediately held Terry's hand under the cold tap and eventually Terry's screams gave way to a dull moaning sound. The teacher sent Marlene down to the office to get help and an ambulance came and took Terry to hospital. All her class sat in the science lab as Mr Cantor was summoned and he tried to find out who had done such a dreadful thing. Marlene knew it was Ewan, although he wouldn't have done it maliciously. She waited, the whole class waited because no one would commit the most serious crime imaginable, that of "snitching" on someone. Suddenly Marlene knew she had to tell. She looked over to where Ewan was sitting and stared at him; he nodded his head as if he knew what she was going to do. Marlene put up her hand and told the Head it was Ewan, but added that everyone who knew Ewan would know that it was just a silly accident. Mr Cantor left the room with Ewan in tow. The class was dismissed by Mr Monger and Marlene went outside to face the music, or, more accurately, the cacophony of a very angry and disgusted class baying for her blood. She suddenly realised that this was how Sidney Carton had felt when he was in the cart going to meet "Madame La Guillotine"

They all decided, her friends reluctantly because they were worried they would be judged with her, that Marlene should be "sent to Coventry". Marlene was surprised how little she cared and carried on as normal. This did not please the ring leaders and, then they said if Marlene was near any of her class, then all conversation should cease. Marlene soon realised that like the never-to-be-forgotten story of "Brer Rabbit in the Briar Patch" this punishment meant she had no more interruptions when doing class work, reading or shooting balls in the break and she was delighted. Unfortunately the class discovered very quickly that nothing they did could upset Marlene's equilibrium and so the episode was forgotten. Marlene was sorry her "punishment" had ended, for now she was interrupted again and usually when it was least convenient. Ewan's part in the "accident" was soon forgotten: he, and Terry continued to be the best of friends; Marlene's friends too, though a little shame faced, were chatting to her once again. She occasionally wondered why she had felt it necessary to spill the beans, but as life went on much as before, she didn't worry about it. Janet found out she had failed once more at the thirteen-plus exam and although her parents were very disappointed, in a way Janet was pleased as she was to stay at the Harpur School with Marlene, Barbara and co.

It was the summer holidays and as usual there were very few girls left in the Home. Marlene decided that they should all play a new game. She had become tired of "Tin Can Tommy" a game where everyone hid except one and then the person who hadn't hidden had to find the rest and, on finding them, one at a time, had to run to the centre of the lawn and kick the can before the person who had been found could kick it. There had been a storm and a very high wind and so there were several sticks underneath the walnut tree and these gave Marlene an idea. She asked Tom the gardener for some string and gathered up as many sticks as she could. The walnut tree was just inside the Sisters' garden, and so off limits for the girls; she quickly carried the pile of sticks to their garden. Armed with string she set to making a bow and with a few straight sticks made arrows. Marlene marked out an area round the swing and started to use her bow and arrows, if that was what you could call such makeshift things. Very soon she was surrounded by most of the bigger girls, who asked her to make them some too and so a very pleasant week or two was spent until she became bored again and moved on to the next thing.

Marlene, Dawn and Bille went for their annual week's holiday in Stevenage. It was strange this time, as Jane's dad, Uncle Paul was home. She had never met him before, indeed apart from Father Count at their weekly confessions, Joe the taxi driver, Jack Nash at the swimming pool and the male teachers at school, she had never spoken to a man before, let alone lived in the same house as one. It was interesting to see the changes in the household. Marlene didn't hear the music which was usually a sign that she could get up; she just heard whispered conversations between Uncle Paul and Auntie Mary. They didn't seem to go out so much, either to "Ga Ga's" or to other houses where Auntie Mary would do the ladies' hair. Auntie Mary seemed busier so Marlene couldn't have her chats in the morning, or indeed at any time in the day. Auntie Mary asked Marlene if she wanted her hair premed. For some idiotic reason, she suddenly thought of Joy, she of the curly hair and the glass eye, and agreed.

One day they were all going on the bus to shop at Hitchin market; Uncle Paul stayed home as he had some work to catch up on, so it was Marlene, Jane, Kate and Auntie Mary. They all sat at the back of the bus on the side seats giving them a clear view of the road. All at once Marlene yelled and they all looked at her leg which was pouring with blood. When all the commotion had died down, Auntie Mary realised that a passing vehicle had run over a large stone and had flicked it through the door of the bus where it had hit Marlene's leg. It was a freak accident, but Marlene was to carry the scar for the next forty years! After the week was ended Marlene went back with proper curly hair, but it was even more unmanageable than ever as no one knew how to look after it. Bille came back with several packets of sweets and tins of condensed milk, which she proceeded to eat all herself during the next few days, much to everyone's annoyance; even Bille's gang looked as if they were ready to rebel, but Bille charmed them back into line.

Marlene had been summoned to the Head Master's office; she tried to think what she had done, but without success. She asked her form teacher, Miss Newbold, if she could go at break, but Miss Newbold was insistent; she must go at once! Marlene knocked hesitantly on the door and Mr. Cantor's deep voice invited her in. He spent a few moments studying her, as if he was surprised at what he saw. He looked down at some papers and then asked her if she was really Bille's sister. Marlene knew she didn't look like Bille, but then she didn't look like Dawn either. She nodded. The Head told her that Bille wanted to move from the "A" class down to the lowest "G" class and asked what she thought about it.

The bottom two classes were divided, so there was a boys' class and a girls' class. Marlene thought for a moment. She asked Mr. Cantor whether he thought he should ring Sister Maud; he said he had and Sister Maud had told him to ask Marlene and do whatever she decided! Marlene and the Head looked at one another in total perplexity.

She thought for a moment and then told him that Bille wouldn't work if she was made to stay in an "A" class and, as it was probable that Bille wouldn't work anyway, she felt, he should put Bille down as she had requested. She told no one of the conversation, not even when her friends asked her why she had been summoned to the Head's office and she certainly didn't tell Bille or even Sister Maude. She still couldn't understand why Sister Maud had made her, and not Dawn, make the decision, but left it there. It was just another unexplained mystery.

Chapter 33: Ballet Lessons and a New Skill.

Pru, who had left St. Etheldreda's two years previously, and been sent to Canada, was now back for a short holiday. Marlene couldn't understand why anyone would want to come back to the Home for a holiday as even Brian Merrill's holidays to Billing Aquadrome would have been more interesting than the Home. However Pru had been having Ballet lesson so she hadn't been in the Home more than a couple of days when Marlene asked her to teach her some steps. Pru couldn't agree quickly enough as she felt very superior: after all, she'd not only gone to another country, but had obviously learnt to dance; a most sophisticated pastime! It wasn't long before Marlene had learnt all the steps Pru knew and Pru, trying to hold on to any advantage she had, told Marlene that you couldn't possibly do ballet unless you had some tights or a tutu. In fact, she said, that she really couldn't teach Marlene any more steps until she had either a tutu or tights. Pru was banking on the fact that by the time Marlene had the said garments, she'd be safely back in Canada and wouldn't have to admit that she didn't know any more steps!!Marlene hadn't a clue what Pru meant; it was clear they were types of clothing, but rather than admit she didn't know, Marlene asked her school friend Janet. Janet told her that a tutu was a special dress, rather like a skating dress that dancers wore when they were performing publicly, and tights were sort of tight trousers, usually black.

Pru went back to Canada after a fortnight and although Marlene still practiced her steps, she felt she couldn't really be a dancer until she had some tights. She thought about it for a few days and eventually went to see Miss Darnell, the seamstress. Miss Darnell told her she hadn't any trousers, as "nice" girls shouldn't wear them, so Marlene went to find Sister Helena-Mary. She listened to Marlene's request and told her to find Miss Guy and tell her that she had spoken to Sister Helena-Mary and it was ok. It was not until the next day that Marlene eventually tracked down Miss Guy and passed on the message. Miss Guy readily agreed to help Marlene, but warned her that if the material was bought, Marlene would have to make the tights! The next week, Miss Guy came looking for her and, with some material and with the aid of a tape measure borrowed from Miss Darnell, measured Marlene. Miss Guy then made a paper pattern, and, arming Marlene with scissors and pins, showed her how to cut out the tights. The material, which was black and quite thin, had been purchased from Braggins , the big haberdashers in town. Marlene was somewhat surprised that Miss Guy should be the one who was giving her all the help she needed, and felt that, maybe, she had been somewhat hasty in her judgement of Miss Guy's character; she felt ashamed that she had not seen any of Miss Guy's finer qualities, but there was still something about Miss Guy that made Marlene a little wary of her.

Miss Guy showed her how to pin the pieces of material together before tacking them. This involved using quite large simple stitches just to hold the garment together to check its fit. Miss Guy had suggested that Marlene should do her sewing down in Miss Darnell's room, so if she needed any help, Miss Darnell was at hand. After Marlene had tacked the tights together and Miss Guy had checked that they would fit, she then she showed Marlene how to hem the seams. It wasn't very long before the tights were done and Marlene put them on and hurried to show Sister Helena-Mary, who was suitably impressed. So Marlene now practised her ballet steps wearing her tights, which was another first for the Home, as no-one had ever made anything except "Dolly bags" at school before. Some people thought that Marlene would now take a real interest in needlework at school but they were completely wrong. It was one thing sewing something you wanted, and quite another sewing something that you didn't choose, didn't want and not only had no use for, but felt was entirely pointless and a waste of everyone's time.

Marlene had noticed that, as Bille got older, she drew people to her in a way Marlene knew she could never do. Bille then held them there by a mixture of laughter and daring. Bille was very impulsive and often took risks, but as it usually ended well, no one really noticed. She was a completely free spirit and she didn't appear to care about anything, always relying on her charm, her unusual appearance, as the only coloured girl in the school, and her mischievous and humorous nature.

Chapter 34: The Birds and the Bees..

It was science again and the class were using their time effectively, though probably without learning much science; Marlene was knitting and reading, confident that Mr Monger would not say anything to her as she was so quiet, and the rest of the class were busy creating mayhem! One of the taller girls who led the class when Marlene was "punished" and "sent to Coventry" came up with a sheet of paper and a pen; she told Marlene they were doing a survey amongst the girls and was Marlene 'on'? Marlene asked her to repeat it, but it made no more sense to her the second time. She thought swiftly and decided not to commit herself fully. She told the girl that she thought she might be; this did not satisfy the girl, who told her she must know, but then shrugged her shoulders and stalked off. Marlene was puzzled, but as it had come from the girls who Marlene had little to do with, she just shrugged her shoulders and went back to her book.

About 6 months later Marlene started having terrible stomach pains, so bad in fact that Miss Howkins confined her to bed. Marlene hated missing school, but her pain was such that she knew she couldn't get out of bed. In fact it was so serious that Miss Howkins made her a hot water bottle, the stone one that Marlene had had so much trouble with so many years ago. After a couple of days Marlene felt better, but a month later the same thing happened. She was lying in bed after dinner when Sister Maud came into the bedroom Marlene and Dilly shared. The house was quiet as all the other girls were at school. Sister Maude pulled up the chair and sat down next to Marlene's bed. Whilst this was happening Marlene was thinking fast, trying to recall if she had done anything wrong. Sister Maude asked about the pain and Marlene explained that, when the pain was very bad, she read so she had something else to think about; she quickly added that of course she couldn't knit and that sometimes if the pain was really bad, she couldn't even read! There was a silence and Marlene said that, of course, she would go to school if Sister Maude felt she was well enough. Sister Maude said nothing, but continued to look closely at Marlene.

This went on for a few more minutes until Sister Maude cleared her throat and Marlene looked at her expectantly. There was some hesitation and lots of "erms" and clearing of throats and then suddenly Sister Maude asked her if she liked keeping her garden. Marlene nodded anxiously, as she thought perhaps Sister Maude would take her garden away, but she really couldn't remember doing anything which would deserve such a punishment. Sister Maude then asked Marlene if she'd ever studied the bees; Marlene said of course and told Sister Maude that she often stroked their furry backs. Sister Maude then told Marlene that the bees gathered pollen from the various flowers which they made into honey. As Marlene knew all about bees, she was totally mystified as to what Sister Maude was trying to tell her and she wondered if Sister Maude was 'of sound mind.' Marlene said nothing, but continued to look at Sister Maude, who then nodded and smiled and then, with an air of complete satisfaction, patted her head and left the bedroom. It was to be years later that Marlene realised that Sister Maud had been trying to explain to her the process of human procreation.

It was the last day of the spring term, a term that Marlene had really enjoyed; she was now a permanent fixture in the school netball team, the only girl to attain such dizzy heights from a "B" class. Some of the other girls in the team were so disgruntled about this that they ignored her completely, except when playing netball, as they had come to realise that when Marlene had the ball, a goal was usually assured. Only one or two girls from the rest of the team actually spoke to her, but this didn't worry Marlene at all, as she was playing very well and she had achieved her aim. Little did Marlene realise how much she had achieved. Apparently when she had first come to the Home, she had been beaten so badly on her back over at least two years that the medical opinion was she would never stand by herself, let alone walk or run. It would take sixty-seven years before Marlene was able to understand why Sister Maud had said, all those years ago, in Mr Norman's office that if Marlene had made up her mind to do something, there was nothing anyone could do about it. This revelation also explained why Marlene could not do certain gymnastics and why she kept having the nightmares concerning her back. Obviously the reason she felt so tired and bruised when she woke, was because she'd been unable to sleep well because of the pain in her back.

It was lunchtime and there was a real upset: Dilly had been made to go over the "horse" at gym. Everyone knew Dilly was absolutely useless at games and her co-ordination was so bad, she couldn't even catch a ball. If she had been in Marlene's class, the accident probably wouldn't have happened, but she was in a class with Lily who had never helped anyone in her life. Anyway, Marlene was wending her way home for lunch when Bille and her gang caught up with her. Five Home girls who were in the same class comprised Bille's gang and, as it was clear to everyone, Bille was the most intelligent and a natural leader, she was the one they all pandered too. The thing that always surprised Marlene was that if any of her gang had sweets from visiting parents, Bille would expect a share, but when she arrived home from Stevenage, sharing was not a remote possibility!

Well, this particular lunch-time all five of them were talking at once, sounding like a group of chattering sparrows, until Bille said she would tell Marlene, because, she said, Marlene never knew what was going on as all she did was knit and read. Bille told her that Dilly had had an accident attempting to jump the horse in gym, the lesson she had before lunch, and that now - pause for theatrical effect - she looked just like a man "down there!". Marlene was absolutely muddled; what on earth did a man look like "down there"? She had never entertained the idea that men were different from women and what they did "down there" was a complete mystery; Bille told her that Dilly wouldn't show them, but ended by saying that she'd show Marlene and if they happened to be with her, well.... It was obvious that there was no "happened" about it: Bille, at least, would definitely be there!

As it turned out, Dilly wasn't at lunch, but Sister Eleanor called Marlene over and asked her to sit with Dilly in the Sisters' room. Bille soon caught on and, with her most angelic look, asked Sister Eleanor if she could go to the toilet. This was something that was not usually allowed, but Bille held her stomach and let a tear roll down her cheek and after all, it <u>was</u> Sister Eleanor. It worked and Bille left the refectory with Marlene, grinning! They caught up with a very woebegone Dilly who, to tell the truth, was secretly pleased with all the attention; she pulled up her gymslip and pulled down her knickers, revealing a large bruise which was so swollen it hung down from her vagina. Marlene examined it, but couldn't see how Dilly's injury had any connection with men at all. Bille nodded knowingly and, although Marlene wanted to ask Bille what the connection was, she didn't want Bille to know she knew things that Marlene didn't; after all Marlene was fifteen months older and knew more about most things than Bille. So that was another "wait and see" problem to be solved at some later date.

Chapter 35: The End of an Era and Marlene Learning to Walk Again!

The Christmas holidays had been and gone when Sister Maude left the Home; the girls had not been told. She was there one day and gone the next as was always the way in the Home. Sister Helena Mary was now in charge and things were very different. Ever since the death of the dog, Bob, they had seldom been beaten, and with the "new broom" that practice was now discontinued altogether. Sister Helena Mary was not as stern as Sister Maude had been, though Marlene always thought Sister Maud had not been as severe as she looked; her stern exterior didn't quite tally with her jokes at the expense of poor Dilly with the butcher and the business with the cockroaches. Now, whenever the Reverent Mother came for a visit from the Mother House in London, the girls used to laugh at the difference in height: Sister Helena Mary barely made five foot, whereas the Reverent Mother was almost six foot. One of the changes was that all the older children could now go into town on Saturday afternoons to spend their pocket money; this was welcomed by everyone, even Marlene, as it meant the house was quiet for at least a couple of hours and she could read her books and knit in peace. As Marlene still owed a lot of pocket money because she hadn't eaten her dinner all those years ago and had wet the bed, she didn't bother going to town; nor did she take time out of her busy schedule of knitting, reading and tending her garden to queue up with the other girls when they collected their weekly pocket money.

One morning in chapel, Sister Helena Mary asked to see Marlene in her office; Marlene couldn't think of anything she had done wrong, so a couple of minutes after chapel Marlene presented herself at the office door. Sister Helena Mary beckoned Marlene in and told her to sit down; Marlene knew this was a good sign! Sister Helena Mary told her that three times a week she would have to go to a clinic in Warwick Avenue to learn how to walk properly. Marlene was rather taken aback; she thought she knew how to walk, but Sister Helena Mary was adamant and so Marlene went to Warwick Avenue on Monday, Wednesday, and Friday afternoons, instead of going back to school. She asked the nurse why she was there and the nurse reddened and said it had something to do with her shoes. Marlene told her that she had only got a "new" pair from the shoe cupboard last month. The nurse hesitated and, after a lot of "ums" and "ahs", asked if the shoes were really new. Marlene didn't understand the question, as whenever the Home girls grew out of their shoes, they just went to the shoe cupboard and got another pair. The nurse asked if Marlene went to a shop for her shoes; Marlene was even more puzzled, as she couldn't understand why someone would go to a shop when there was a perfectly good shoe cupboard. The nurse then said that because the shoes didn't fit properly, she had to do lots of exercises to make her feet better.

Although Marlene still wasn't sure exactly why she had to do the exercises, she quite enjoyed them; she learnt how to pick up pencils with her feet, even attempting to write with them. She loved running and jumping on a bar and generally saw the whole thing as just another challenge. After six months the nurse told her she needn't come any more, but as Marlene could have told her that before she went, she didn't ask what, if anything, had improved! Sister Helena Mary said she'd done well, but what it was she had done, she hadn't a clue. She still went to the shoe cupboard when her shoes didn't fit anymore, so really, in Marlene's view, the clinic had just been a welcome break from the tedium of her life.

Chapter 36: Criminals All? A Taste of Teaching.

Marlene's thirteenth birthday came and the summer holidays were approaching fast. One Saturday, just as lunch was finishing, Sister Helena Mary came in with some men. Everyone was quiet and still. There was an air of foreboding and Sister Helena Mary looked even sterner than Sister Maud used to look, if that was possible. She asked the smaller children to leave the refectory, which they did in absolute silence, and then looked at the girls who were left. Sister Helena-Mary told them that a great number of them had been stealing from Woolworths and asked them to put up their hands if it concerned them. The girls looked round hastily, but Sister Helena Mary explained that the gentlemen with her were policemen and they knew which girls were responsible. Five minutes or more went past, during which Sister Helena Mary and the policemen stared at the girls. Then all hands went up except Marlene's. Sister Helena Mary and the policemen stared at Marlene, but Ethel and Moira told them Marlene hadn't joined in with anything and was probably reading, knitting or both. Dawn's hand went up last and there was lots of muttering and pushing around her, but she still kept her hand up. Sister Helena Mary asked all those who had raised their hands to go and get their "ill-gotten gains".

Dawn looked very worried and left having an urgent and spirited discussion with Moira. Marlene was sent out, but she heard later that Dawn hadn't gone to Woolworths either. Dawn, apparently had been going to Tinsley's riding school in Clapham, every Saturday afternoon without permission. Marlene couldn't believe it: Dawn riding! She was totally bemused. Why anyone would want to disobey Sister Helena-Mary just to see or even sit on a horse, she couldn't imagine. Moira had told Sister Helena Mary the truth. Dawn was sent for and she was told she could go to the riding school on Saturday afternoons and that she would also be allowed to take lessons. The girls who had stolen goods were not allowed to go out for two months and were given extra jobs to do on a Saturday afternoon. It was clear they had learnt their lesson: "If you do steal, don't get caught!" Marlene couldn't understand why they had stolen make-up and cheap jewellery, as they couldn't wear it and anyway it would be taken from their rooms when they were at school, as everything always was. It was after Marlene had left the Home that she was told that Maggie was considered a saint by her "Deaf and Dumb" club, as she always brought hundreds of things for the Christmas Bazaar! That was obviously the fate of all their Christmas and birthday presents and anything else the girls were given.

Marlene was writing a play; she had read somewhere that Shakespeare had written a play which was called "The Scottish Play" and as they had a kilt in the dressing up box she decided that she too would write one. She begged paper and pencil from Sister Helena Mary and was busy for the next week, feverishly writing. When Marlene thought she had finished, she took it along to Sister Helena Mary to get her approval to raid the dressing – up box and start rehearsing. Allocating the parts was a minefield; people such as Moira had to be given the best parts, as did Bille. As far as Moira was concerned, Marlene knew if she didn't get a good part, she would be very angry and an angry Moira was dangerous. Bille was a different matter, as if she didn't get the best part, none of her gang would participate, and, might even sabotage the play. Dawn got a singing part as Flora Macdonald singing "Over the Sea to Skye" who then died a heroine's death in the closing scenes. All was set fair; rehearsals were going well. Marlene had the part of the hero who had to fight Moira, a wicked Scotsman who had betrayed the others to the English. Then disaster struck: Moira gave a very enthusiastic swing of her "plaid" and a picture of, appropriately, Highland Cattle came crashing down. They were all stunned; Marlene went straight to Sister Helena Mary who was furious and as a result all the contents of the dressing up box were thrown in the bin. Marlene didn't write any more plays and the whole thing was soon forgotten by everyone except her.

Sister Helena Mary had asked to see Marlene. She had now lost any dread she once had at receiving such a summons and went straight away. Sister Helena Mary started talking about Kate, who should have left the Home at 15, but hadn't. The nun explained that Ethel's and Kate's mother had died when they were still young and that was why they had come to the St Etheldreda's. Marlene remembered seeing their father who often came to the Home to take the girls out. Apparently their father had promised their mother that Kate should have the opportunity to have nurse's training, and have it while she was living at the Home. Sister Helena Mary had moved Kate to the only single bedroom and she asked Marlene if she would help Kate with her studies. Marlene was taken aback and protested she knew nothing about nursing, but Sister Helena Mary insisted, saying, Kate would take notes and Marlene would test her on them. Marlene wasn't sure, as she never really listened or worked hard in class; most of her attention was focused on the latest book from the library or, if she was lucky, her knitting. However she thought it might be interesting and so she agreed and she soon learnt all the important bones in the body, as well as lots of other facts which she felt, whilst interesting, were of no real value to her. It did, however give her a taste of teaching and although she really couldn't see how she could ever teach, it was still very much in the back of her mind.

Chapter 37: A Taste of Heaven...Then Reality and Then There Were Two!

In late September Sister Helena Mary sent for Dawn and Marlene, telling them to go to Miss Darnell and ask for their best clothes. They were both a little mystified, as neither of them knew they had any "best" clothes. However, Miss Darnell gave them both dresses which had only just been given to St. Etheldreda's by the "great and good" so they hurriedly changed, brushed their hair and shined their shoes. Sister Helena Mary gave them the "once-over" and told them to walk to St. Paul's Vicarage. She gave them directions and they were told to ask for "Granny Count" as they were having afternoon tea with her. Marlene was mystified: what was the difference between "afternoon tea" and the bread and jam tea they had as their last meal of the day at 5'o'clock.?

The two girls walked quickly and were soon knocking on the large and imposing front door. Mrs Count opened the door and directed them upstairs, where they were to knock once on the door facing them and go in. They had seen Granny Count at church very occasionally, but they had never spoken to her and so, they were completely taken aback at this unexpected outing. Granny Count seemed the archetypal grandmother with white curly hair and a round girth. She walked with a stick, as she couldn't stand upright and had difficulty walking; she welcomed them and soon both girls were at their ease.

Granny Count showed them some of her "things" which were very old and very precious; apparently even her own granddaughters were not allowed to play with them. She had a very strange music player, with a turntable and funny solid metal rings, which had spikes sticking up from them; these spikes caught on the music player and created the tune. Marlene was fascinated by them. She had beautiful small porcelain statues of birds. Mrs Count always looked very aloof and seldom spoke to anyone, but Granny Count was very different with her twinkling blue eyes and her merry smile. Marlene loved her on sight, even though she was obviously a lady and one of the "great and good".

Granny Count explained about the very old strawberry patterned plates they were to eat from and told them how to check if they were genuine. Apparently they were all hand-painted and the strawberry pattern had a faint mark which was where the artist had begun and finished painting. She let them wind up and listen to the very old musical box, which played beautiful music Marlene had never heard before; this wasn't surprising, as the only music she had ever heard was either church or chapel music or, very occasionally, music on the radio in St. Andrews, which was the sitting room for the older girls. Granny Count also introduced them to her cat, Lei, a Siamese cat like the ones in "Alice through the Looking Glass", who made the most extraordinary noises which Granny Count said was her way of talking.

All in all it was a perfect afternoon. They had melon for tea and Granny Count taught them how to eat it, and there were very small sandwiches cut into triangles and lovely cakes. It reminded Marlene of that far off tea she'd had at Miss Richards' house all those years ago and she wondered briefly if Granny Count was going to adopt her or Dawn, or perhaps both. Then Marlene thought she'd have to adopt Bille as well and, although Bille was quite grown up, she really couldn't see anyone wanting to adopt Bille as you could never really depend on her to be good when it mattered. Marlene then wondered whether she was right and Granny Count wanted to adopt, but only one of them, so it would be her or Dawn. At that moment, Marlene suddenly realised she no longer wanted to be adopted: she had ready access to books and she could rely on Sister Helena Mary supplying her with wool and needles and in the summer she could go swimming every Saturday afternoon. No, she was content with her life. Dawn, however, wasn't; she loved the riding lessons, but Marlene felt that it wasn't enough for her; perhaps nothing would ever be enough!

Marlene sought permission from Granny Count to ask her a question. She had read that in Victorian families the first son went into business, the second into the church and the third into the army and she wondered if that was the case in Granny Count's family. Dawn shot a furious glance at Marlene, as Dawn, who probably also had visions of being adopted, didn't want Marlene to spoil her chances, but Granny Count didn't seem to mind; she told them her first son, Richard, managed the Poppy farms in Africa, her youngest son, Steven, was in the army and John, Father Count, her second son had gone into the church. This fascinated Marlene, who asked if her boys minded that they didn't have a choice. Granny Count smiled and said it was tradition and whether they minded or not didn't have a bearing. Soon it was time to go and, although the girls still didn't really understand why they had been invited, they'd had a great time; Marlene, however,. was still convinced they were there for a form of test that had something to do with adoption. After they'd arrived home, Marlene thought about Father Count; she always had the strongest feeling that he did not like being a priest and she also realised that even having money and position meant you were probably not free to follow your dreams. Even the "great and the good" could be trapped in a system which disregarded individual choice.

The months went by and one day Marlene awoke with the pain again, but this time there was blood. She was ashamed of dirtying the bed and, after carefully covering the blood-stained sheet so no-one could see, she ran to find Miss Howkins, who told her she would have the pain and the blood every month. Marlene didn't like to ask why and anyway, she had been taught from the age of three that you didn't query anything you were told, but just accepted it! Miss Howkins took her to Sister Eleanor, who gave her a pad of material which looked like cotton wool and an elastic belt. Sister Eleanor explained that when that pad was very dirty, she had to throw it in the boiler in the scullery, and then find her and she would give her another one. So this was the pattern for the next few months.

Marlene was cross: every evening when she settled down in St. Andrew's to read and knit, Moira and Dawn turned off the light. She then heard little giggles and sighs, but couldn't think what they were doing. Someone was always by the door to switch the light on if they heard a member of staff coming. When Marlene asked Dawn what they were doing, Dawn just said Marlene wouldn't understand and even if she did, she couldn't play because "You're not big enough." Marlene asked in vain what Dawn meant, but she wouldn't say. It wasn't until years later and after she left the Home, that Dawn told her, but even then Marlene couldn't see that touching each others' breasts was remotely interesting!

As Christmas approached, Dawn stopped Marlene in the corridor and told her she had to go into service at the Counts. Marlene didn't understand what Dawn meant; she had read books where poor girls had to go into service , which was a nice way of saying they were servants, but surely Dawn didn't mean this? Dawn said that was just what she meant. Marlene was quiet, as although she was very conforming on the surface, she knew when she left the Home she couldn't bear being told when to get up, when to go to bed and what she would be doing every second of every day. She was saddened because she had thought that she and Dawn were invited to Granny Count's to assess them to see if they were suitable for adoption; she had never dreamt that Granny Count was only being nice to them because she wanted to know if Dawn would make a good servant. Obviously, Marlene thought bitterly, Dawn was considered good servant material! Christmas was upon them, but this year Marlene had seen the reality of life: her sister was only considered fit to be a servant and a live-in one at that. Marlene wondered what fate had in store for her. She certainly would not make good servant material! However Dawn didn't seem to mind and she left the Home for good soon after New Year. And then there were two: just her and Bille.

One of Dawn's duties was to escort the Count girls' home for lunch; they went to school at the High School, the same school Marlene should have gone to if she hadn't doctored her eleven plus. It seemed ironic that the eldest of the Count girls was less than a year younger than Dawn, but Dawn had to see them safely home. Although she saw Dawn every day there was seldom any time to say anything except "hello" and "goodbye". Dawn had some photos taken of her: a lot of little square photos for not much money. She also joined the Bedford Operatic Society, but Marlene didn't think Dawn would be there for very long. The society was known for its members being mostly drawn from the "great and good", and Dawn couldn't tolerate them. True to form, Dawn told Marlene three weeks later that she didn't go any more.

Dawn was no longer at the Count's; she knew this, as Dawn didn't meet the Count girls out of school, but Marlene was not concerned. Because St. Etheldreda's Home was organised by age groups, Marlene sometimes didn't really talk with Dawn for weeks on end even when they were living in the same house, so even though Dawn wasn't in the Home any more, Marlene wasn't worried nor was she missing Dawn in any way. Years of seeing girls there one day and gone the next meant that Marlene wasn't capable of forming strong relationships, not even with her sisters. Marlene was completely institutionalised! It wasn't until Marlene was sixty-nine that she had any information as to where Dawn was when she left the Home or what she was doing.

Chapter 38: Marlene in Real Trouble and Rosie's Sudden Disappearance .

Marlene now had the best bedroom in the Home. Kate had left and was in training at the hospital and Dilly had left the Home suddenly, again without notice. Marlene was now taking girls' disappearances in her stride, but she did occasionally miss Dilly who, for all her lack of initiative or brains, had still been a good friend to her. She thought about Dilly's mum with her silly shoes with "stilts" on them instead of proper heels, her huge red lips and the "Home Made "chocolates she used to bring. She could understand a little why Dilly only gave Marlene a quarter of one chocolate and kept the rest for herself: poor Dilly seldom had any way of gaining any status within either the Home or school and the chocolates meant that for a brief time she was popular. She was important!

A film called "The Robe" had opened at the Granada. Marlene remembered seeing huge posters announcing the opening of the cinema when she hadn't been at the Home very long, but as they'd never even thought they would ever go, a cinema remained outside her experience or interest. However as "The Robe" was to some degree about the life of Christ and was also concerned with the birth of Christianity, all the older girls at the Home were to go. All week Marlene had been looking forward to it and, after lunch on the Saturday, the girls dressed in their Sunday attire. Rosie's bedroom was next door to Sister Eleanor's and Marlene's and, while Marlene was getting dressed, Rosie came in to her bedroom. She started pushing Marlene, first in jest, but gradually harder. Marlene asked her to stop, but to no avail, and in the end Marlene warned Rosie that if she didn't stop she would bite her arm till it bled! Marlene was as surprised as Rosie when she heard herself threaten Rosie in this way, but once she'd said it she knew she'd have to go through with it.

There was quite a long pause, with both girls unsure what to do; it was a long time since Marlene had had to threaten someone, either with a look or an action. Rosie pushed her again and Marlene, hating herself all the time, bit down hard. It didn't break the skin, but it bruised almost straight away. Both girls stared at each other in shock, then Rosie started crying and Bille, who shared a room with Rosie, heard her cry and dashed in to Marlene's bedroom, closely followed by Miss Hawkins. Both girls were sent to Sister Helena-Mary's office to hear their fate. Rosie told Sister-Helena-Mary the whole story and tried to protect Marlene, explaining that she had been warned. Marlene knew she was in the wrong as she should have just walked away. The upshot was that both girls were told they must miss the film, which considering it was the only film they were ever likely to see, was the ultimate punishment. Strangely enough, neither girl seemed particularly concerned and Marlene, who knew she could have made things worse for her, went out of her way over the next week to be more thoughtful to Rosie.

Marlene liked being in a bedroom on her own, as, if she waited until after Sister Helena-Mary had finished her rounds, she could put her light on and read; strangely enough, even when Sister Eleanor, who slept next door, caught her with her light on, punishment had not followed. Sister Helena-Mary went round all the girls' bedrooms last thing at night and, as Marlene was always awake, she often stopped to ask her about her day. Marlene was tempted to tell her of her dream of being a teacher, but Kate had been the only one to have stayed on at school, after she was fifteen, and that was because her father had decreed it. Thinking about it, Marlene wondered whether Kate had wanted to be a nurse or whether as it had been her dead mother's wish; perhaps Kate, like Granny Count's sons, had had no choice in the matter; maybe it wasn't just the "great and good" who were tied to outside influences when it came to careers. Certainly Dawn hadn't had a choice, even though she hadn't stayed very long at the Counts' house.

Rosie and Marlene, who were now fourteen, were allowed to go to St. Paul's Church youth club, which was along the same road as the Home. However, Rosie had other ideas: she'd arranged to meet some boys outside the youth club and asked Marlene to keep a look out while she and three of the boys went down a nearby alley. Marlene hung around for a short while, but became bored and went into the club. Marlene really enjoyed the youth club and had learned to play table tennis. As was usual when learning a new sport, she quickly became very adept. At first the boys at the club, who usually hogged the table tennis table couldn't be bothered to play with a beginner, but, as the weeks went by, they realised that Marlene, unusually for a girl, could be counted on to give them a good game. There were very few girls at the club, as it was St. Paul's Church youth club and most of the girls in church came from the St. Etheldreda's anyway. The few girls there didn't go to her school and Marlene felt she had nothing in common with them, as all they seemed to do was giggle and talk in whispers. Marlene had already recognised most of the boys, as they were all choir boys who went to the "posh" private schools; the girls went to the High School, the very school that Marlene had decided was not for her all those years ago. With so few girls, Marlene felt she wasn't too out of place with her long grey socks and second hand clothes and, as she was usually to be found either playing table tennis or keeping score, she didn't have to mix with her own sex at all.

It seemed to be just like school break time as Rosie didn't come into the club at all, but suddenly appeared when the club closed and Marlene was walking back to the Home. A few months later Rosie seemed to be getting fatter; always a big girl, she had put on so much weight that even Marlene noticed. Rosie was one of the few Home girls who wore a brassiere and just lately her brassiere seemed to be far too small. Marlene wondered, briefly, why Rosie didn't tell Miss Howkins so she could get a bigger one but, as Marlene usually had her nose in a book or was clacking away with her needles at every opportunity, she never got round to mentioning it to Rosie and, as no one else seemed to notice, Marlene soon forgot all about it. It was not long afterwards that Rosie suddenly disappeared too, although her sister Peggy was still in the Home. This was unusual as most of the girls who left the Home went back to their families and of course their sisters went too. Marlene was the only "Home Girl" left in her year, but as she had friends in her class, she wasn't concerned.

Chapter 39: Marlene Broadens Her Activities.

It was early afternoon on a Saturday in early October and Marlene had finished her book. Although she had another to start, she usually liked to have a break between books to think about them and so was in the rare position of having little to do. The other girls were in town, but Marlene didn't see the point of looking round shops. She remembered Dilly's obsession with clothes shops on that far off day Dilly had taken her to school in the wheel chair, but she still couldn't understand why anyone would want to keep up with the latest fashions.

As Marlene was wondering what to do, she had an idea: she would cook! Marlene was not particular good at cooking in school so why on earth she thought she would be able to cook anything by herself, heaven only knew. Having made up her mind, she went off to find Sister Helena-Mary. The nun listened to Marlene's request and asked her what she would like to cook. Marlene was stumped as she hadn't thought that far ahead and then remembered that once, when she was at Janet's house, she'd been given a biscuit; she'd never had one before or since, but she remembered they'd been very nice and so she said she'd like to cook biscuits. Sister Helena Mary thought for a moment, and then asked her if she would like to cook cheese biscuits for the Sisters' supper. Marlene jumped at the chance and followed Sister Helena Mary down the stairs; the stone stairs where, long ago, she'd refused to stand aside and had dared Ethel to push her down them. Marlene remembered she'd won then and every battle afterwards.

When they arrived at the big familiar kitchen where all the inhabitants of St. Etheldreda's had stirred the pudding and where the older girls had peeled apples whilst singing her anthem, Sister Helena Mary had a few words with Maggie and then went back upstairs. Maggie was a little bemused as no girl had ever done any cooking before, but produced a very battered book. Marlene looked through it carefully, but only found a recipe for sweet biscuits.

"I have to make cheese," she mimed to Maggie, who just looked at her and then said, "'eese." Then, with a series of gestures and grunts from Maggie and wild guesses by Marlene, she understood that she had to leave out the sugar and replace it with cheese. Maggie showed her where all the ingredients and the cooking utensils were and Marlene rolled up her sleeves and began what was to be a life-long hobby. After about an hour, with Maggie watching every move she made, they both tasted her cheese biscuits straight from the oven and then took one or two of the still hot biscuits to Sister Helena Mary for a taste test. It was a good thing Marlene had only taken two biscuits, as they disappeared very quickly. Marlene took the plate to the scullery and caught Maggie also sampling more of her biscuits, leaving only just enough for the staff to have two each. After that, Marlene was often summoned to the office and asked if she could make biscuits either for the Sisters' supper or when the "great and good" were paying a visit.

After the success with her biscuits, Marlene looked around for something else to learn. She had seen Sister Eleanor playing the piano and thought that it might be interesting to learn. Although she hadn't given it any real thought, she assumed she could pick it up as quickly as knitting and cooking, however, after four weeks, she realised it was a much bigger commitment and that, apart from three lessons a week, she would have to practise daily. So Marlene decided it wasn't for her.

Chapter 40: Another Battle and Bille to the Rescue!

Dawn had been gone well over a year now and Marlene was now fifteen. She was in her last term at school and Mr Cantor had announced at the beginning of term who were to be Half-Prefects in their year. This meant you had green braid sewn half way round your blazer and helped the teachers supervise areas of the school at break and lunchtime and between lessons. Marlene noticed that all the names read out were from the "A" class and so decided to go and see the Headmaster. This was the third time that only the "A" classes had been allowed to do things that other classes couldn't participate in. Marlene hadn't done anything about the "Hansel and Gretel" play, but she had made sure that Miss Flitwick could not leave her out of the school netball team and so she decided to go into battle once more.

She knocked on his door and, when he invited her to come in, he seemed very surprised to see her. Marlene asked him why she had not been made a Half-Prefect and he replied that of course she had been considered, but wasn't she "staying on" next year? Marlene looked at him in amazement and had a sudden rush of hope, before realising that she didn't have a father who insisted that she stay on, like Kate, and so of course she would have to leave. She explained this to the Head and, after looking at her very doubtfully, he told her that in the exams her class had just taken, she'd come second in the whole of the year. Marlene thought for a moment, but realised that this information didn't alter the fact that she still didn't have a father and so she reluctantly told him that she didn't think she'd be staying on. Marlene also told him that she didn't think it right that only the "A" classes should be considered suitable material for Half-Prefects. Mr Canter asked her why; she thought for a moment and then said that just because they might have more brain power, this did not mean that they were more responsible, did it? It was therefore no big surprise that Wanda, who was half Indian and the most sensible member both of Bille's gang at the Home and of her class at school, was made a Half-Prefect the following year.

At the next assembly the Headmaster asked all the Half-Prefects to come up one at a time. As they went up, he spoke a few words to explain why they were being given this honour. When it was Marlene's turn, he spoke about her academic ability, her tenacity in practising netball shooting every day and her swimming ability which had helped her "House", "Cowper", win the swimming trophy. More importantly, however, he stressed her sense of what is right, and remarked that even he had been put in his place by Marlene's sense of justice.

However, a few months later an even stranger thing happened; Marlene needed another sanitary towel and so went to find Sister Eleanor only to be told by Sister Helena Mary that she was out for the day. Marlene explained that she needed a clean pad, but was told she would have to wait. She was really upset, as she badly needed a clean pad. Bille passed her and saw how upset Marlene was, and, as Marlene was rarely upset, asked why. Marlene told her and Bille looked at her for a while and then asked if she could keep a secret. Marlene assured her she could and so Bille opened a drawer in her bedroom and showed Marlene about a dozen pads hidden under the clothes. She told Marlene she always collected a few more than she needed, as she too had needed one sometimes when Sister Eleanor was out. Bille told Marlene that if she had any more problems of that nature, she could just go and help herself. Marlene was amazed at how clever Bille was to have planned in advance the solution to a very difficult problem, and how kind Bille was to help her out in such a way. It wasn't until a few months later, after Marlene had left the Home, that the real reason for Bille's "generosity" was made public knowledge or, at least, public insofar as some of the older girls knew.

Bille and Marlene went to Stevenage again for what was to be Marlene's last visit while living in the Home. It was also Bille's last visit but at the time no one realised it.

Chapter 41: Prefect Duties and That Nightmare Again!

Marlene was wearing her blazer with the braid on which showed all and sundry that she was now a prefect, albeit only a "half" prefect; she was admiring herself in the shop windows on the way to school. Marlene was the only one in her class to be a prefect and, before school, had wondered whether there would be any comments, but she need not have worried as her class had long since ceased to be surprised at anything she did. Mr Canter called all the new prefects together and explained their duties. Marlene was to be on duty at break time on the stairs and Mr Canter stressed that she should be on the look-out for pupils running up and down the stairs, as well as infringements of uniform. He seemed to be very worried by boys' fluorescent socks, though how on earth she would be able to see what colour socks the boys had on was beyond her! Marlene was also concerned that other pupils wouldn't take any notice of her; after all, she didn't think she would take kindly to someone her own age telling her what she ought to do.

A few minutes before break time saw Marlene positioned half way up the stairs and it wasn't long before a gang of boys burst out of a classroom upstairs and came shouting and running, almost tumbling, down the stairs. Bravely, Marlene stepped into their path and, in as level a voice as she could manage, politely asked them if they would walk upstairs and then walk down quietly. There was a silence and Marlene stood her ground and pointed upstairs. To her amazement, the boys did exactly as she'd asked them and this taught Marlene a valuable lesson: if you are in authority and have to ask someone to modify their behaviour, you must look as if you expect them to do as you ask. Having a few yards of braid on her blazer gave her authority and her body language merely reinforced it.

By the end of the first week Marlene was not exactly enjoying the experience, but hadn't had any of the problems she had envisaged. To her surprise she had seen one boy wearing fluorescent socks, bright green in fact; the only reason Marlene had spotted them was the boy's trousers, like those of many boys in the school, were too short. Money in the early fifties was still hard to come by and most of the school's catchment area consisted of very poor, almost slum dwellings, and so trousers had to be worn as long as possible, even if it meant that said garments were really too small! Little did either of them know it at the time, but this was the boy she was to marry! Marlene sent him back up the stairs and told him that on this occasion, she wouldn't report him. Marlene felt satisfied with the way she had managed and it did not go unnoticed, as Mr Canter summoned her to his office and congratulated her on the way she went about her duties, quietly and confidently. Marlene missed practising goal shooting but, as the school didn't play netball in the summer and she was leaving school in July it didn't really matter one way or another.

Marlene woke up tired and sore. She'd had that nightmare again! A man had been chasing her with a pneumatic drill, the sort that men use to break up concrete or dig holes in the road, and pushing it into her back. It was strange: any other dream or nightmare she had was always gone by the morning and there were no after-effects. However, whenever she had this horrid recurring dream, Marlene woke up with a very sore back and was extremely tired, almost as though it had actually happened. This would continue for the rest of her life.

Chapter 42: A Surprising Gift and Actually Shopping for a New Dress

One late evening, when Sister Helena-Mary was making her nightly rounds, coming last to Marlene, who was always reading. although "lights out" had been announced by Miss Howkins at least half an hour ago, she sat down on Marlene's bed and held out a small box. She told her to open it and inside was a gold ring with Marlene's initials, M.P.G, on it. She was lost for words, especially when Sister explained that her own mother, Mrs. Gibson, the lady she and Dawn had stayed with at Maryport all those years ago, had given her on her fifteenth birthday. She went on to say that she and her mother had discussed it and, as she wasn't allowed to wear it, they both felt Marlene should have it. Sister Helena-Mary urged her to try it on and in spite of the difference in stature, the ring fitted. Sister Helena-Mary then said that if Marlene still wanted to be a missionary, she must save at least a hundred pounds by the time she was eighteen and then she could go to college to train. Marlene had never been quite sure that she wanted to be a missionary, but as she had three years to decide, she supposed she could change her mind, though at that moment it seemed very improbable! Next morning, Marlene wondered whether she could wear the ring to school, but wasn't sure whether it was allowed and so, fatefully, left it behind. On her return at lunchtime, the ring had gone, just as every birthday present and Christmas present had disappeared after a day or two. Marlene didn't have the courage to tell Sister Helena-Mary and, if she had noticed that Marlene never wore the ring, she didn't mention it either; however Marlene never forgot her kindness.

Marlene was summoned to Sister Helena-Mary's office one morning with Lori, a girl who had arrived at the Home only a few months earlier. Sister Helena-Mary told both girls to go to Miss Darnell who would give them some "new" clothes after which they must report back to her, washed and tidy, within the next twenty minutes. When they were ready, Sister Helena-Mary gave them the "once over" and then hustled them out of the front door. As they walked towards the town, she told them she was going to buy each of them a new dress, ready for when they would leave the Home in a month or so. They finally arrived at a small shop, where Sister Helena-Mary had a whispered conversation with the manager who called out to a shop girl to bring two dresses which she thought would satisfy Sister Helena-Mary's criteria. The girls were shown two green dresses trimmed with black velvet; one had a small black "peter pan" collar and the other had a small belt trimmed with black. Marlene didn't like collars but, as Lori immediately grabbed the other one, she had no choice. They tried on the dresses and showed them to Sister Helena-Mary who seemed pleased. She didn't ask Marlene and Lori what they thought, and the purchases were paid for and parcelled up and that was that!

It was a only a matter of days later that Sister Helena-Mary, again on her nightly rounds and visiting Marlene last, sat down on her bed. She told Marlene that she was to leave the Home in a month's time and she had found a choice of jobs that Marlene might like to do. Sister Helena-Mary told her that one was at the Cadena Bakery which served a very posh cake shop and cafe on the High Street; the other choice was a market garden and nursery just out of town. She didn't want an answer straight away and she said she would leave Marlene to think about it.

Chapter 43: Shopping For More Clothes and a Decision Made

It was at this time that Marlene was again summoned to Sister Helena-Mary who told her that for the next few weeks she was to be given seven shillings and sixpence to spend on clothes. As someone who had no interest in clothes whatsoever, except for the wonderful dress that she had worn to Mrs. Richards' all those years before, Marlene had no idea what to buy, but that Saturday, armed with her first seven and sixpence, she set out. She wandered around, eventually ending up at the top of the High Street, and in the window of Richards was a skirt: it was a tiered and very full green skirt with big white spots. Marlene cautiously went inside. A shop girl came over and asked if she could help and Marlene pointed to the skirt. "Yes, Madam, what size?" asked the assistant.

Marlene had no idea but, as the girl looked kind, Marlene explained that she had never bought any clothes for herself before or indeed had any shop bought clothes, so she really had no idea of size. The shop girl looked at her curiously, and so Marlene found herself telling her all about the Home and the green dress, which she didn't like. She also told her that for the next five or six weeks she would have seven and sixpence to spend on clothes but, after that time she would have left the Home and would then have to pay for board and lodging, so the clothes she bought would have to last her for the foreseeable future. Marlene also told her she liked the green skirt in the window. The shop girl, having looked appraisingly at Marlene and guessed she was probably a size fourteen, fetched the skirt in that size and, apart from being rather big round the waist, it fitted perfectly. Then the girl had an idea: she told Marlene to choose a blouse, even if at that moment she didn't have enough money, so she could try both on to see how they looked together. Marlene chose a white, finely knitted cotton top, with what Tina, the shop girl, described as a "boat" neckline. They looked lovely together, but, before Marlene could say anything, Tina asked Marlene to wait a moment while she had a word with her manager.

Tina came back with a very elegant lady who asked Marlene if she would like to hear a proposition that Tina had thought up. Firstly, Mrs Brown, the manager, went over Marlene's story very carefully and then said that if she would like to, Marlene could choose matching clothes and, if she didn't have enough money at the time, then Tina would make sure that the garments were put to one side for her. She also informed Marlene that, as she would be buying several garments, the shop would give Marlene ten percent off every garment. Tina, the manager went on, had also thought that perhaps Marlene wouldn't want to buy everything from the same shop, and that was fine too. The manager also told Marlene that just this once she could take both the blouse and skirt home there and then. Marlene couldn't believe her good fortune and, not wanting to take advantage, gave Mrs Brown the telephone number of the Home so that she could verify Marlene's story. Mrs Brown laughed and said she didn't need to do that, as she knew all about St. Etheldreda's Home and the only proof she needed, she could get just by looking at Marlene! Marlene wasn't quite sure what to make of this, but was so pleased with her purchases and the kindness of Mrs Brown and Tina that it didn't really impinge on her.

So that was the pattern for the next few weeks. Marlene had been excused Saturday duties and so every Saturday morning she made her way to Richards' dress shop and, even if Tina was busy with a another customer, Mrs Brown called over another shop girl, freeing Tina to serve Marlene. In fact it wasn't really just serving as Tina also gave her a great deal of advice on clothes and also confided in Marlene that she really envied her figure. This caused Marlene to look critically at her body, but the only thing she noticed was that her breasts were smaller than her rib cage; it therefore became her ambition that one day her breasts would be larger than her rib cage.

Every Saturday afternoon would be spent at the swimming pool; Marlene was becoming a very strong swimmer and she revelled in the water. One Saturday afternoon she was at the baths on her own when some girls, who Marlene was on nodding acquaintance with from school, started shouting and screaming: a gang of boys had started throwing the girls' towels in the water. Marlene quickly got out of the water and, grabbing the rest of their towels, went back into the pool. Holding them above the water with one hand, she swam into the centre of the pool and stayed there. At first the boys thought she would become tired and drop the towels, but they hadn't reckoned with Marlene's extreme stubbornness and after fifteen minutes or so they became bored with the whole thing, allowing Marlene to return the towels to the girls and carry on with her swim. As she still couldn't bring herself to dive, it became almost a point of honour for her to jump off the top board every time she entered the pool, although it still rankled that she was scared of diving. This problem would have to be addressed at a later date.

Chapter 44: School's Out for Summer and an End of Childhood.

With the term nearly over Barbara and Gill asked her what job she was going to. They asked her if she would like to be a telephonist, as if so, they would all be together. Marlene hadn't given a thought to what she wanted until Sister Helena-Mary had given her a choice. Marlene wanted to be with her friends, but recently Bille had decided she wanted to be a telephonist and even now was busy learning all the codes for the towns and cities in England. Marlene hadn't realised that every town and village had a telephone code, but she knew that she shouldn't spoil Bille's dream. Bille wanted to be the first girl at St. Etheldreda's to be a telephonist. Marlene also was amazed that Bille was already planning her career a whole year ahead as well as knowing that there was such a job as a telephonist. She also knew that she had been lazy and unrealistic by not giving any thought to her own future. Marlene still had teaching at the back of her mind but, because it was unattainable, hadn't bothered to think any further. The jobs Sister Helena-Mary had chosen for her were very appropriate, considering her interests, but they had been Sister Helena-Mary's choice, not hers! So reluctantly she told her friends that she had a job already: she was going to work at a bakery.

Marlene remembered the careers interview she'd had and the embarrassing silence that ensued when the man conducting the interview got no replies at all to his questions. But what could she have said? Marlene was institutionalised and had no idea what, if anything, she wanted. As to what she was good at, besides reading, knitting and baking biscuits, she had no idea; no one had ever praised her or talked to her about whatever talents she may have had. In the end, after a quarter of an hour's long silence, he dismissed her with a cheery "Good luck," though why she needed that she hadn't a clue. Marlene remembered far off days looking for a four-leaf clover and trying to catch a leaf and knew she wouldn't get the luck that everyone, including all the teachers when they said goodbye and the Head at the final assembly, seemed to think she needed. So Marlene left school and looking back she saw she had achieved much; she had two firsts and a second in the school sports'sday; firsts in triple jump and long jump, probably because she had taught herself to "fly" down the stairs in an effort to save time, and a second in swimming. She had made the school netball team and, if Miss Flitwick was to be believed, was the best "shooter" Miss Flitwick had seen!! So although Marlene did not want to leave school, she could do so with her head held high

Her friends asked her if she would like to come to the school dance. Marlene thought about her new green skirt and white blouse and knew she would look all right, but was worried that she really didn't know how to dance. Marlene knew that the few ballet steps she had learnt would not suffice and, as she'd never seen anyone dancing, except occasionally pictures of people dancing together in pictures in books, she really hadn't a clue. However, her friends had been kind to ask her and so she asked Sister Helena-Mary if she could go. She was surprised when the nun gave her consent, and delighted when Janet asked Marlene if she'd like to come to her house for tea, so they could "get ready together". Marlene wondered why they would need to "get ready" together; after all, it didn't take a minute to put a blouse and skirt on, but as Janet had so kindly asked her, she said she would ask Sister Helena Mary. Permission was granted and so, with her new clothes in a brown paper bag, the two girls walked to Janet's house after school. There was a delicious tea and then afterwards Marlene was initiated into the "girly" word of make-up, hair dryers and rollers, and all the other paraphernalia that goes into getting two "Cinderellas" ready for the ball! Janet's mother seemed as excited as Janet and, although Marlene enjoyed the novelty of the occasion, she did feel it was rather a waste of time, as, with make-up on and her hair curled, even though she could see the difference, she wasn't sure she liked what she saw.

Janet's father escorted them to the dance. The dance was quite a surprise, with the girls standing at one side of the room and the boys the other. All the girls were dressed in either lovely full skirts with belts nipped in at the waist and blouses, or in pretty dresses and the boys looked as if they had had a good wash. It was amazing how different everyone looked out of school uniform. Ewan asked Marlene to dance and they stumbled round the floor together. When the music changed to a very loud up-beat song so did the dancing. Couples were now standing on their own, opposite each other, and jigging up and down in time to the music. Sometimes they held hands and swung away from each other. Marlene was hooked! Then Terry came over and asked Marlene to dance this new dance and, although she had never even heard the music before, Marlene soon picked it up and really started to enjoy herself. It was soon time to go and Janet's father was waiting outside to take the girls home; he dropped Marlene off first and then left to take Janet home. It was nearly ten o'clock; Marlene had never been up so late before and after saying good-night to Sister Helena-Mary, who had stayed up especially to see her before she went to bed, Marlene fell into bed and slept heavily till morning.

School Photo 1956

5th row: far right, Donna; 5th row, 4th from right, Bille

6th row: 2nd from right, Marlene, Wanda 2nd row 3rd left

Mr. Cantor, the Head, far left; Mr "Jack" Williams, far right.

Chapter 45: Another Invitation and a Reality Check

Marlene and Lori were summoned to Sister Helena-Mary's office one Saturday lunch time. Sister Helena-Mary told them they had been invited out for tea the next day. Marlene knew it could mean one of two things: either they were being appraised with regard to adoption or they were being assessed as to whether they were good "maid" material. However, when she thought it through, neither seemed plausible; she was surely too old for adoption and Sister Helena-Mary had already told her to choose between two jobs. Marlene was puzzled! The next day the girls set off together. Marlene didn't know Lori, but the little she'd seen hadn't impressed; Lori seemed loud and had a silly laugh, which she used on every occasion. Marlene longed to ask her what she thought was so funny, but years of living in a community had taught her not to rock the boat unless it was absolutely necessary.

The directions they had been given took them the whole length of The Embankment and, as it was a Sunday afternoon, all the "great and the good" were promenading, wanting to see and be seen! Marlene had been told the house they were visiting was just round the corner from The Embankment; when they arrived, Lori rang the bell. There was a huge hydrangea in a pot by the door and, when the door was opened, Marlene's attention was on the plant, rather than the lady who opened the door. They were shown into a small hall; at least it was small compared with the Sisters' hall at St. Etheldreda's. The lady, who introduced herself as Mrs Stevens, then showed them into a small dining room and they were directed to sit at the table where a lovely tea was laid. There were very thin sandwiches without crusts, trifle and a chocolate cake. It really was a sumptuous tea. Marlene was mystified as to why they'd been invited. There was an older lady there as well, who Mrs Stevens introduced as her mother. After tea they were shown into another room with a sofa and chairs laid out. Marlene and Lori sat down and were asked numerous questions, all of which seemed banal. There were two dogs in the room and so

Marlene's attention wandered as she stroked the dogs and left Lori to answer the questions, only joining in the conversation when a question was directed solely to her.

After about an hour, Mrs Stevens indicated that the visit had come to an end by telling the girls she had to get ready to go to church and so Marlene and Lori left for the long walk home. Lori asked Marlene what she had thought about the visit; Marlene told her that she felt Mrs Stevens preferred Lori and that she hadn't a clue why they'd been invited. When Sister Helena-Mary did her round that night, she asked Marlene about the visit. Marlene admitted that she'd found all the questions they'd been asked boring and pointless, but she also said she felt Lori had been a hit! A week later, Sister Helena-Mary told Marlene that the reason they had visited Mrs Stevens' house was that she was looking for a lodger and after the visit had decided that Marlene would be ideal. Marlene was amazed, for her instinct told her very clearly that it was Lori, not her, whom Mrs Stevens had warmed to. Later Mrs Stevens' mother told her that her instinct had been correct, but it was she who had wanted Marlene.

Marlene's departure from the Home was imminent, but she still hadn't decided on her job. After a lot of thinking, she realised the answer was purely a practical one. Marlene went to Miss Darnell and asked her what clothes she could take with her. Miss Darnell said in addition to the clothes she had bought, Marlene could also have three pairs of pants, a swimming costume, two very small brassieres, two "liberty bodices", two pairs of socks and one pair of shoes. No winter coat or jumpers were available, except the one she had knitted. It was now clear which job she would take. Marlene loved the idea of becoming a gardener, but knew that without winter clothes or any form of transport it would not be possible and so reluctantly told Sister Helena-Mary that she would take the job in the bakery; she reasoned that she would be warm, it wasn't so far to the bakery and if she couldn't afford to pay for her meals, at least she might be able to eat at the bakery for free.

The next Saturday morning, knowing she only had one more week's money for clothes, she told Tina at the Richards shop of her predicament, namely that she would need some sort of jacket. Tina promised to look out for one and Marlene asked her how much a jacket would cost. Tina told her to save what she was going to spend as two weeks' money should cover it. The last Saturday before Marlene left the Home, true to her word, Tina had found a jacket in another shop in town and had permission from Mrs Brown, her manager, to go with Marlene to see it. It was a camel colour, quite light-weight, and fitted Marlene. Although Marlene was not in raptures over it, she did see it would be useful during the winter and, as she would have six shillings left, Tina suggested buying a cardigan she's seen in another shop. After they'd made all the purchases, Marlene thanked Tina for her kindness and then walked back to Richards to thank Mrs Brown also.

In the afternoon Marlene made her way to the swimming pool, she thought perhaps for the last time, for she was very aware that the only money she could rely on in the future would be what she was able to earn and she was realistic enough to know that there would be little enough of that!

Sunday dawned and Marlene went to church, again possibly for the last time; she felt completely alone and very apprehensive. During the service she made no attempt to join in the prayers and hymns, even though she knew the words. Questions kept going round and round in her head: how would she know how to look after herself? What about cooking and how would she wash and iron her clothes? What did she know about how to behave in a real home? Yes, she had some inkling from what she'd learnt at Auntie Mary's, but Marlene also knew that a week's holiday once a year could hardly compare with lodging with someone for the foreseeable future. She also felt very strongly that Mrs Stevens thought she was second best and wondered whether that would be a problem. Marlene also worried about money; she knew she would have ten shillings over each week after she had paid Mrs Stevens, but it would have to stretch an awfully long way. There would be sanitary pads to buy, toothpaste, soap and socks or stockings for the winter. If she bought stockings she would need a suspender belt so perhaps stockings would not be possible! Marlene was told she would have to start work at six-thirty, but had no transport; she would have liked to buy a bike, but knew she would have no money to do so. She could walk, but would have to allow more time. As she only had one pair of shoes, she wondered what she would wear if they needed mending. How would she be able to afford a new pair if they wore out? All these problems seemed to be insurmountable. In the Home, she had taken for granted that there was always company if she wanted it, but how would she cope at being on her own?

She recited the collect for the last time, even though Sister Helena-Mary said there was no need and slowly ate her dinner. Marlene ate silently, ignoring the buzz of the girls' chatter around her. Dinner seemed to be over quickly and with the air of one who was facing an execution, she went upstairs to pack the meagre supply of clothes in the case Sister Helena-Mary had given her. There were no personal items except for her comb and a small amount of make-up: some eye-shadow and lipstick that Bille, in a rare moment of generosity, had thrust into her hand. Marlene turned and walked downstairs for the last time.

Chapter 46: Alone!

After saying her goodbyes to Maggie, Miss Howkins, Sister Helena-Mary, Sister Theresa and Sister Eleanor, Marlene left by the Sisters' front door and walked slowly into the summer sunshine, hampered by her new suitcase. She felt unreal; surely this wasn't the end, just this? She was walking away after twelve years, the "goodbyes" and "good lucks" ringing in her ears and she just walking away. She struggled down the imposing front steps, which were wide and white, curving to embrace, enfold the front door.

Marlene passed the arid flower beds where the snowdrops clustered thickly on dark January days, but lay barren for the rest of the year. She remembered....but that was yesterday, last week, last month, last year. Now she was free, now she could walk where she liked, do what she.....but what could she do? She passed her tree, the Plane tree which was visible from several points around the small market town. She remembered....but she had to look forward to an exciting adventure, a future, but of what? Thirty girls and several staff had always surrounded her....Well, it seemed like always and now, here she was, completely alone.

She had gone to bed with the other girls, been woken by the bell with the other girls, had breakfast, gone to church and had dinner all with the other girls and now she was alone, completely alone! She'd never been really alone, never made any real decisions, not even about the sort of job she wanted, unlike Bille! What was she to do? How would she know what to do?

Marlene reached the gate and slipped through it and, as she was shutting it, looked once more at the place that had been her home for the past twelve years: a home, a prison, a place to flee to from the jeers of derisive school children delighted to have someone more unfortunate than themselves to mock; a place to flee from to the freedom of academic work, such as it was. Now she had left and so, squaring her shoulders, she set out on the long journey to Mrs Stevens' house and an unknown future.

3402312R00125

Printed in Great Britain
by Amazon.co.uk, Ltd.,
Marston Gate.